LIVE WHAT YOU LOVE

THE DEFINITIVE GUIDE TO INTENTIONALLY IMPROVING YOUR LIFE, HOME, BUSINESS AND FINANCES USING CREATIVE FENG SHUI.

SARAH STONE

authors
AND CO.

★ ★ ★ ★ ★
'Putting the Creative into Feng Shui. Pure genius'
Kathryn Cowan

★ ★ ★ ★ ★
'Creative Feng Shui is my new way of life. Read it, Do it,
Live it.'
Lucy Crane

★ ★ ★ ★ ★
'When self-empowerment meets this book, magic
happens'
Chelle Shohet

★ ★ ★ ★ ★
'Refreshing and makes so much sense'
Kimberley Banner

'Finally… a book on Feng Shui which I can actually understand'

Lucy Crane

'The new generation of self-help has arrived'

Samantha Meijer

'Pure magic, helps you create intention and love in your life'

Ally Davis

DEDICATION

I'm dedicating this book to those who have felt a little lost on their pursuit of success in life, love, business and more, this is for you.

You are not alone, everything you need is within you.

You just need to find your way…

CONTENTS

I AM
COMMITTED
TO LIVING
WITH
INTENTION

INTRODUCTION

**I see the beauty in life,
I feel the heart of a home,
But most of all, I live what I love.**

Welcome to one of the very best kept secrets for life transformation and self-empowerment, I am so excited to share this revolutionary experience with you.

Creative Feng Shui provides you with the opportunity to live with intention, transform your emotional, physical and financial experiences of life, encapsulating the components of your mind, body and soul. The best part? You're currently holding the very 'how' in your hands.

Sounds like a BIG promise... doesn't it?

As your Intentional Living Expert and Certified Creative Feng Shui Practitioner, it's my aim to help people all around the world to create profound transformations in their life, business and finances. Helping others achieve their version of success has always been my passion, and I am now able to share my 25 years' work / business experience, intuitive knowledge, skills and dedicated expertise in this unique concept, throughout this book; I get to help you to identify what is blocking you from living limitlessly and then show you how you can intentionally style your life so that you are positioned for success and abundance.

When I was first introduced to Feng Shui, the first question I asked was *'what exactly does Feng Shui mean?'* and I'm sure if this book is your first insight into this ancient art of living, you're probably thinking the same, so let's start by turning to an entry in the dictionary:

Feng Shui- n. *A Chinese art which is based on the belief that the way you arrange things within a building, and within the rooms of that building, can affect aspects of your life such as how happy and successful you are. Believed to bring good fortune.* **Origin-** *Chinese, from Fēng 'wind' and Shuǐ 'water'.*

— ~COLLINS ENGLISH DICTIONARY –
COMPLETE AND UNABRIDGED ©
HARPERCOLLINS PUBLISHERS

The term 'Feng Shui' actually translates to wind (*Fēng*) and water (*Shuǐ*) and more importantly, in alignment with the Chinese Culture, is associated with 'Good Health' and 'Good Fortune' which I think we all deserve more of. My intention is to guide you through some specific techniques throughout this book so you can proactively and instantaneously invite better health, more luck and improved prosperity into your life.

Creative Feng Shui is an effective concept for deliberately structuring our lives. This book will help you learn the practical magic and ancient wisdom of Feng Shui so that you can apply it to modern life and utilise this proven artform of activating this energy system into your living and workspaces. By doing so, you can activate dramatic and life-changing results which help to:

- Increase the positive energy flow in your home, life and business.
- Rapidly dissolve any energetic blocks that have quietly held you back for years.
- Turn your workspace into a magnet for abundance, success and productivity.
- Experience joyful and harmonious interactions with others in your living or work spaces.
- Turn your living spaces into three-dimensional vision board of your optimal life.
- Accelerate the rate of success with your personal development and growth practices.

- Transform your home into a focal point of unconditional love, connection and health.
- Amplify your manifesting power by harnessing the energy of your surroundings.

The way we live is drastically changing and having the ability to balance and enhance the energy in our environment is one of the most powerful things we can do to create more peace and harmony in our lives, whilst still actively pursuing our goals and desires for the future. Because the spaces where we live, love and work are a reflection of ourselves, they have the power to enhance our lives too. Excitingly, using the methodology of Creative Feng Shui, we can tap into this powerful energy system and magnify our potential.

Whilst I may not have all of the answers within this book, I know by the end you will start living with intentional alignment and have the ability to implement these powerful techniques into everything you do for real life-changing results.

WHEN SERENDIPITY STRIKES

For as far back as I can remember, I've always wanted to create a life of my wildest dreams. To travel the world, meet inspiring people and to experience amazing things. I've always wanted to continually learn, develop, and make a positive contribution to the world. And I'm sure I'm not alone in this.

Learning how to create a better life is something I've always been passionate about, and it took the milestone of turning 40 for me to join the dots and make me realise my true purpose. Prior to this, for many years it felt like I was constantly searching for the missing piece of the puzzle, seeking fulfilment in trying new things, launching new things and helping others build their aspirational life and business.

The problem? I was so busy prioritising everyone else and doing everything for everyone else, I forgot about my own dreams. I had no boundaries. No vision, no goals, and I started to completely neglect myself in more ways than one. I was basically telling the Universe that I didn't matter so 'go ahead and prioritise everyone else'.

Over a period of time my health deteriorated, and I was feeling exhausted, lost, alone, sad and broken. Burnout set in, the panic attacks started, and I found myself withdrawing more and more. My confidence was at an all-time low, and it took hitting rock bottom to realise that I was destined for bigger things and definitely made for more than THIS.

Something had to change. My husband, Andy, could see I had lost my sparkle and he just wanted his wife back. He wanted me to be happy again, but I didn't have an ounce of happiness within me, and that's hard to admit without acknowledging how much sadness I had manifested.

At the time, it felt like I had no right to be unhappy. I was in a loving marriage, we had moved to a beautiful part of New York, and we were travelling around the country experiencing incredible things, but I wasn't adapting well to change, and I was a world away from embracing the life available to us. I needed to heal. I needed to look within and make some significant changes but didn't want to go down the route of medication or other methods which I didn't feel aligned with.

I'm extremely fortunate to have an inner circle of professionals, business colleagues and friends to call upon and it's thanks to these friendships and loving relationships, along with the unconditional support from Andy, which helped pull me through the lowest point in my life.

I returned to the UK riddled with anxiety and not knowing where to turn. At the time, my Mum was also very poorly in hospital, so my first priority was to be by her side and be there for her. Thankfully she made a recovery, and we were able to stabilize her in her home.

Serendipity started when I received a call from my friend, client, soul sister and real-life guardian angel, Nichola Sproson. Nicky is the founder of an incredible healing technique called the 'Intuitive Alignment Model,' and we had previously planned a photoshoot on my last trip to the UK, but it didn't work out, so her call was to see if I had availability to do her photoshoot in Glastonbury, England. Everything aligned, and within a week we were on our way to the sacred home of healing.

From the moment we arrived, I knew this was exactly where we were supposed to be. Shortly after we arrived, I found out that I had been taken there not for a photoshoot, but for two days of intensive intuitive alignment healing; my very own 1:1 retreat in the most magical place in the world. It's without doubt the kindest, most loving, caring and powerful show of compassion which I will never forget and feel forever indebted.

A vision and memory I will never forget is standing at the top of the Tor, one of the most spiritual sites in the country, feeling a transformational energy so powerful and being overwhelmed with emotion, a new-found love for myself and an abundance of forgiveness for those who had hurt me in the past. It was like the biggest weight had lifted from my detoxed mind, body and soul.

I healed and my intuition was awakened. I had reconnected with myself and got into complete alignment in the most empowering and uplifting way. The whole experience was life changing. If you ever have the opportunity to experience something of this nature, embrace it. I personally think everyone at some stage in their life should experience this rejuvenating, re-energising and enlightening 'New Beginnings' treatment as it could help make the world a better place.

With this renewed energy, there was a significant shift, and the anxiety vanished. I had been given the tools to heal, make space for new beginnings and fresh perspective on my reality.

I had the opportunity to live life in any way I choose to and guess what? YOU get to do the same.

Shortly after my retreat in Glastonbury everything started to change. The next major epiphany was at an event I had been flown into the UK for, to photograph a women's weekend, Destined For Bigger Things. This phenomenal event was organised by my friend, client and confidant Kezia Luckett, Positive Psychologist and Founder of Women of Contribution. Held at the stunning Wotton House in Surrey, this event brought together a collection of some of the most successful and inspiring women making a positive impact on the world.

The keynote speaker was globally renowned Feng Shui Master Teacher and the well-known star of the worldwide phenomenon "The Secret", Marie Diamond. Over the two days and in an intimate setting, I was given an insight into the world of energy and Feng Shui and I was hooked.

This was my missing piece of the puzzle. I was destined for bigger things, and Feng Shui was to play a major part in the next phase of my business and personal development.

I returned to New York like a new woman. Every single day following that special weekend has included learning Feng Shui guided by Marie herself and other industry experts, implementing Feng Shui, teaching Feng Shui and living Feng Shui.

When I was first introduced to Feng Shui, I remember feeling uncertain and scared that I might get it wrong. However, the stories of change that I had heard and witnessed from others were so great that it encouraged me to lean in further as the results were phenomenal. I decided to tune into my intuition and ask myself, my divine guidance, to clearly 'show me how'. If I ever did something wrong or I was on the right track, it wasn't long before I discovered that my path was 'meant to be'.

I had just completed my certification in Feng Shui and was questioning (doubting) myself, 'can I really do this, am I on the right track, show me show...' and in that very moment as my husband and I walked along the same beach we visited every week, our eyes homed in on a large coin, sparkling in the sand, proudly waiting for us to pick it up. Our reaction was 'WOW', and even my husband was impressed with the serendipitous treasure we had received.

There is no doubt that this was a message, specifically at the time I needed to hear it. The coin was a Chinese Laughing Buddha with symbols on the back. When we researched it further, the coin is known to bring good luck, contentment and abundance into one's life. It depicts plenitude of whatever one wishes for – be it wealth, happiness or satisfaction. Marie's reaction was 'WOW' too, and this powerful response to my question was the reassurance I needed to pursue my new-found path of creating Creative Feng Shui.

Since then my learnings have flowed, my energy has been transformed, unexpected opportunities have presented themselves, and here I am writing a book for you about Feng Shui so that you can invite more luck and abundance into your life too.

I share this story with you now to encourage you to be open to the magic that can take place following on from the changes you make to reposition your life. So be bold and have the courage to put your intentions into action.

Now, I want to share what I've learned with you.

One of the most important things that I've discovered is how powerful it feels when you become intentional on how you want to uniquely 'live what you love'.

What do you want to do with your life?

Why were you put on this earth?

What is it that gets you out of bed in the morning?

Where would you like to take your future life, business, relationships?

What are your wildest desires to really live the life you love?

What do you need to change to make all of this happen?

Knowing what you want out of your life is the key to creating your intentional life. This isn't about dreaming up a real-life fairy tale. It's about creating a life you desire, so that you can live in abundance and make those desires your reality.

There's also never been a more poignant time to create a better environment to support how we live and to make a contribution in making the world a better place to live, love and 'be'.

My ultimate goal is to introduce you to more peace, harmony and flow in your life and business by sharing the art of Creative Feng Shui so that you can instantly apply these practical tips, tools and advice to help you take inspired action to pursue your full potential for success and happiness in every part of your life.

I AM CONSTANTLY WORKING TO ACHIEVE MY GOALS

HOW TO USE THIS BOOK

TRACK YOUR PROGRESS

Agood solution for the written exercises and all the notes you may want to record is to use an intentional journal or a notebook. This will help you track your progress and ensure they are easier to find when you want to look back on these findings in the future. Make sure that it has plenty of pages so that you can keep all your visualisation intentions and goals, all in one place. I have specifically created a range of products which may help with this, and you can find those, along with a collection of resources, on my website at www.sarahstone.com.

Diarising and acknowledging what you notice will become a vital part of your momentum. The stories, the windfalls of abundance, luck and synchronicities will all cultivate an unwavering belief in the power of Feng Shui and belief in your ability to create and live your boldest dreams attaining your biggest goals and vision for yourself.

SEEK AN 'INTENTION BUDDY'

Having someone to share your experiences, and encourage you with your intentions, activations, and results will motivate you to do more and give you more confidence in achieving the success you deserve. If you don't have an intention partner yet, support them in bringing him/her up to speed with your desires. Share this book and work through the activations together. As you do, you will tap into the power of collaborative learning which, in turn, will accelerate your immersion into the process of learning and fruition of your results. A creative virtual partner is just as effective so don't worry if right now you haven't got a partner as you are invited to join us in the Creative Feng Shui Society where you meet like-minded people from around the world who are all collectively supporting each other in this friendly space. You can find out more about this in the resources section at the back of this book.

TAKE INSPIRED ACTION

It's important to reassure you in these very early stages that there are no wrong answers here, this is your safe space to be honest with yourself, to dream big, to visualise your future, to make intentional changes for the better and to be open to how Creative Feng Shui can enhance and improve your life.

To take the most value from this book, delete the word 'perfection' from your vocabulary as NOBODY IS PERFECT. By taking inspired action (imperfect or not), you are at the very least, starting the change of energy flow and something is better than nothing. The smallest changes can instantly start to reposition the positive flow of energy, and the aim is to build upon that gradually.

You are in the driver's seat here, and there is no need to get overwhelmed with any aspect of the process. You will be encouraged to make small, simple and frequent changes as these small shifts can make a massive impact, so if something doesn't feel right, you have the choice to change it at any stage.

THE '111' FORMULA

Behind every successful person is their ONE Thing.

Possibly one of my all-time favourite books is 'The One Thing' by Gary W. Keller and Jay Papasan. The book discusses the value of simplifying one's workload by focusing on the one most important task in any given project.

This book was a game changer for me and has had a huge impact on how I live, work and show up, so I want to incorporate an adaptation of this methodology to help simplify the process we'll work through to incorporate Feng Shui into your life.

The '111' formula breaks down to intentionally taking action: 1 day to do 1 thing for 1 hour to get extraordinary results. I can personally recommend using this successful habit-forming process because no matter how you measure success, personal or professional, only the ability to dismiss distractions and concentrate on your ONE thing stands between you and your goals.

There is absolutely no expectation or requirement that every element of this book needs to be applied in to your life all at once. In fact, I personally recommend that you prevent overwhelm by practising the process of intentional living by following this formula throughout this book and see how this methodology compliments your inspired action taking towards the bigger picture of your optimal life plan.

This concept alone will transform how you can become more intentional in everything you do. Give it a go; I can guarantee it will help you be more productive and gain more momentum in whatever you focus your efforts towards.

THE MAGICAL '999'

You may be intrigued to know how long everything takes before you start to feel and see the effects of Feng Shui? Well, every situation and person are totally unique, and therefore it would be impossible to give you a specific date. That said, there is huge significance to the number 9 in Feng Shui as it represents the culmination of a cycle with events reaching a pinnacle and self-mastery.

Once you know your power positions, you've started to activate and enhance these areas (which you'll learn how to do in this book), the effects could be instantaneous, they could take 9 hours, 9 days or even 9 months for more significant changes.

The number 9 is something you need to look out for - so start to become aware of your surroundings, numbers, dates and times because some results can manifest instantaneously as an outcome of good Feng Shui.

To give you a clear perspective on how this shows up in your life, it can take as little as 9 days for the easier activations to start flowing, 9 weeks for the bigger changes to start taking effect and 9 months for the more significant life changes to start flowing.

It's important for you to know that the time it takes for your activations to take effect strongly relies on your own commitment and consciousness. In other words, the more you work on your energy, the faster the results will happen. It could take nine seconds, nine hours, nine days, nine weeks or nine months to have the changes work for you and your life. Look for the signs of change and celebrate as they start to take effect.

TAP INTO YOUR INTUITION

Use this book however you feel guided to use it. You can binge read it in one go, or you can flip to the section you feel you want to focus on in your life right now. You can also open the book randomly and see what message comes your way. Most importantly, you should use it in a way which feels right for **you** because this is your personal 'luck book' and you can do whatever you like with it.

The intuitive power is within you to know what you need to do with the information shared within these pages. At the back of this book, you will find a glossary of Creative Feng Shui terminology and phrases referred to throughout the book so if you need a more detailed explanation, make sure you head there.

Take your time. We're all so different, and it's best not to make too many changes too quickly, so look at focusing your intentions towards one specific area before moving onto the next. Making changes in this way allows you to see and feel what's working for you, and I've found that this approach has seen quicker success for my clients.

Consider involving an intention buddy in the process of incorporating and activating Creative Feng Shui as it's so rewarding, fun and exciting to share your experiences as we go through these powerful practices. When this starts working for you, it's like watching magic and miracles happen before your very eyes - so share this real-life treasure hunt with someone special.

Allow this book to inspire you, but don't allow it to dictate or overwhelm you. The aim is to 'let it flow' and 'let it go'.

You can access the books accompanying resources, tutorials, free audio guides, worksheets and more over at www.sarahstone.com/book-resources, so, make sure you head there so that I can support you further throughout this book.

I AM
INVITING
LIMITLESS
PROSPERITY

WHAT IS CREATIVE FENG SHUI?

Creative Feng Shui is a practice that intentionally prioritises the energy of our surroundings and ourselves in specific ways. Under its influence, we can invite positive synchronicities of attracting the right people, opportunities and 'luck' at the right time and place.

Creative Feng Shui is ultimately a self-improvement-meets-self-empowerment practice which allows you to develop a way to interact with your environment through energy and how it feels so that you can consciously create a positive flow within you and around you so that you can get more of what you want. Happiness, harmony, health, wealth, better relationships, fame, recognition, balance, creativity, joy, connection, collaboration.... you get the idea.

Our homes, offices, gardens and favourite spaces have a huge influence on our lives and how we feel, so by utilising these vital connections, Creative Feng Shui will become the tool you can use to change those things that influence you most and therefore, also change the way you feel.

Once we start to create this positive flow of energy, we can then harness it to enhance any environment. Your space, wherever that may be - is powerful. Activating your surroundings with intention is your secret to unlocking a whole new way of living and attracting what you desire.

My personal experience of Feng Shui has been 'insightful' and it's the reason I'm writing this book and why I've developed Creative Feng Shui as there are lots of different ways to shui! Fortunately, through learning these different techniques and working through the more sometimes contradictory elements of do's and don'ts, I've found my own way to shui that works and is SIMPLE, yet extremely effective.

I've purposefully added the word 'creative' to Creative Feng Shui because creativity is the physical act of turning new and imaginative ideas into reality. By combining this with the powerful practice of feng shui, the straightforward approach produces a perfect storm of creative energy, action, intention and flow to consistently keep you moving towards more of what you want so that you can live what you love.

I firmly believe that your creativity is your secret weapon and that we are ALL creative in some capacity. It's true. Sometimes we have a very narrow view of what being creative is because when we think about being creative, we imagine ourselves painting a landscape with oil paintings, taking a poetry class, fashion design of clothing or capturing the perfect portrait. These are excellent examples of the power of creativity, but not the only ones. Creating something can be as simple as preparing a meal, writing a handwritten letter, scaling your business or renovating your home. The key is that you are tapping into your mind, body and soul to make or produce something in your own unique way, and THIS is what is at the heart of Creative Feng Shui.

It's probably best if I break Creative Feng Shui down into its simplest form. It's really about understanding and influencing the positive balance of energy into your home and to your life. Like anything in life, for consistent results, this is about a lifestyle, not a one-time application. We now know that everything around us is energy (also referred to as Chi), our thoughts included, so it isn't surprising that this ancient art and science can impact every area of your living and presence. When we are able to tap into and combine the energetic changes with physical and psychological ones, we are cultivating a powerful force which inevitably will result in everlasting effects.

Creative Feng Shui is also about wholeness, not parts. Everything is alive, connected and changing all the time. So... if something is not working for you, change it. If something doesn't feel right, change it. If something isn't bringing you joy, change it. Our intuitive sensibility will let you know if something doesn't feel right and if something isn't aligned with your energy flow (shui), it will have an impact on every area of your life in some capacity. Simple. Trust yourself and don't be afraid of making these changes because when you find your flow, that's where the magic happens, and momentum will start to flow (which is your indication to do more and keep doing what you're doing).

Together we're going to use the energetic frequencies of thoughts, colours and objects to activate the flow of Chi and remove stagnant Chi throughout your home and workplace so that you can create an abundance of positive energy which will build momentum and empower you to actively live the best life possible.

Creative Feng Shui is not a complex concept, and so it has never been easier for the modern world to leverage its power and for it to bring dynamic influence into your life. One note to remember here; it is important to recognise that the power of Creative Feng Shui is impacted by the attitude of the individual and everyone brings a unique presence to their environment. For example, if a person has great Feng Shui in their home but no goals and a terrible attitude, his/her results will be ineffective. I invite you to take responsibility for approaching this with openness, confidence, belief, trust and a positive attitude towards the energy of yourself, others and your home.

This powerful concept is not one to be mistaken with a 'magical manifestation' experience, and I'm hoping by now after understanding a little bit of the history and science behind it, you are appreciating the magnitude of how powerful it can be for achieving life-changing results. Understanding the five elements of the Life Cycle is also going to be a focus for this next chapter as I know it will empower you to make slight changes for quantum results. There is also a powerful connection between these five elements, the life fields and your personal energy number, all of which, when applied together will significantly support you in creating real balance and successful cycles of flow.

Don't let the terminologies and the relationships to their meaning overwhelm you. I will be introducing you to the concepts of Wind and Water, Yin and Yang, Positive Energy, different kinds of luck, animals, your personal energy number, the five elements, the 'magic map' and the nine fields of life; success and money flow, personal and professional relationships, health and wellbeing, collaboration and partnerships, creativity and joy, new beginnings and life's journey, helpful people and travel, wisdom and inspiration and finally balance, peace and harmony. It will all become clear and easy to embrace as we delve a little deeper so sit tight, trust in the process, 'shui with me' and I eagerly await your results to present themselves as you start uncovering your personal Creative Feng Shui success secrets.

Get ready to delve into your psyche, discover your intentions, get into alignment, learn how to tap into your intuition, unlock your roadblocks, reach your goals, create your limitless success and seek your fortune.

Ready? Let's dive in.

I AM
READY TO
RECEIVE

HOW IT WORKS

I t is said that everything in our life is created via three levels of manifestation. Feng Shui Grand Masters call it the 'three levels of luck' and when you come to understand the different strands of luck, you can identify the level of change you can create.

In Creative Feng Shui, the foundations of good fortune and luck are based upon three types:

Heavenly Luck
Human Luck
Earth Luck

Heavenly Luck is the first kind of luck which is associated with the life and circumstances you were born in to. It's attached to your place of birth, time of birth, parents, race, culture, talents, hereditary patterns, circumstances and chance. It creates up to 1/3 of your overall luck which comes from your birth destiny, and it is said that heavenly luck is relatively difficult to change.

Human Luck is formulated from your attitudes, habits, thoughts, and behaviours that determine what you do with your life's circumstances. Therefore, what you decide to do with the circumstances you have been given determines what kind of Human Luck you can expect to enjoy.

This type of luck creates up to 1/3 of your overall luck and is driven by the choices and changes you make along the way as well as the quantity and quality of your actions. It, therefore, requires discipline and overcoming habits that no longer serve you.

Earth Luck is determined by the positive or negative influences of your environment. This type of luck is, by far, the simplest to change and is directly influenced by the principles of Creative Feng Shui.

Creating up to 1/3 of your overall luck, when you are aligned with the positive and prosperous forces that already exist within nature and the environment that you live in, you are sending a strong message to the universe:

'I AM READY TO RECEIVE'

So, now you know where 'luck' comes from, the next step is to combine this knowledge with the 9 major life areas which are found within traditional Feng Shui.

These 9 fundamental life areas form 'The Bagua Map' which I like to refer to as 'The Magic Map' and this powerful grid can be transferred, overlaid and applied in everything you do. Your land, your home, your room, your desk, your website, your brand and even your car! It focuses on:

Wealth & Abundance
Fame & Recognition
Partnerships & Collaborations
Family & Friends
Creativity & Joy
Helpful People & Travel
Career & Life Path
Knowledge & Self Cultivation
Health & Wellbeing

Each of these self-explanatory areas affects the corresponding area of your life, home and business. The secret technique of Creative Feng Shui is to further enhance these areas of our life by also combining them with the five elements of nature (our environment) to complement, enhance and activate change through:

Fire
Earth
Metal

31

Water
Wood

These five elements define how Chi energies interact with each other and feed, calm, give life to or destroy each other. These powerful cycles are similar to an atmosphere that you might experience at a certain time of day and in a particular season of life.

To use Creative Feng Shui as your tool, to combine all of the luck, focus and action, we the make the process personal to **you** by tapping into your heavenly luck to access the energy archetype you were born with.

Kua numbers (*aka* your magic number / your personal energy number) is a numerical system based on your date of birth and gender. It determines your more fortunate directions to face, work in and maximises the opportunities to increase a better flow of energy by attracting more positive outcomes for everything you desire and more.

The methodology of Feng Shui translates this invisible energy into a personal energy number. This number then gives you the opportunity to identify the four most prominent directions that are considered more fortunate for you.

According to more ancient Feng Shui traditions, every degree in your environment (all 360 of them) will create a different outcome. Therefore, in any room or space, this

Feng Shui compass will tell you exactly which directions to focus your energy and intentions on.

This technique simplifies the process immensely and provides an insight as to why these four ideal directions can then be found on a compass:

South
South West
West
North West
North
North East
East
South East

The power of these prominent directions is uniquely significant for all of us and are used to further enhance 'The Bagua Map' and focused energy for what you want to attract.

The final stage of this powerful process is to direct all this abundance of energy to the right area of your life so that everything aligns and flows effortlessly and easily for you. To do this, simply set your intentions for what it is that you want to 'call in' by setting some very specific intentions for:

Success & Money Flow
Personal & Professional Relationships

Self-Cultivation & Personal Development
Health & Wellbeing

Once you know what your personal and professional intentions are, where the energy needs to be focused and what you want to achieve, all that is left to do is take inspired action, *every single day*.

If you're wondering 'how on earth am I going to do *all* that!?', don't panic! Throughout this book, I'll be guiding you through how you can bring each of these significant area's into balance, harmony and flow so that you can then activate and enhance its effectiveness with ease. It is my intention to become your tour guide as you start out on this new pathway to understanding the method behind the intrigue of Creative Feng Shui.

Since the start of my obsession with Feng Shui, I've been asked many times by friends and colleagues, "what are you up to with this 'fengi-sway-thingy' and what is it all about?" … at this point, I imagine many of you may still be wondering how you even pronounce the word in itself. Feng Shui, Feng Shu-y, Veng Shu-y… not quite! You can pronounce it 'Feng Shway' is probably the easiest way to break this down but quite honestly you can say it anyway that makes sense to you – there's no judgement here!

As you now know (unless you were naughty and skipped the first few pages), the term 'Feng Shui' translates to Feng *(wind / energy)* and Shui *(water / fortune)*. When we think about wind, we know it's a movement of air. You can't see it, but you can feel it and see how it affects areas of your life – just like energy. Water, on the other hand, is visible and relates to the outer environment. You can see it, you can touch it, and you can direct its flow – just like your fortune. This is how they both work in complete synchronicity.

There's something I want to ask you now that I consider us friends in the safe space of these pages… are you actively creating the life you choose? I mean REALLY creating a life you love?

If not, don't worry, you will receive the tools to change your circumstances. If you are, amazing! We'll go even further to create more of what you desire.

This book will be your opportunity to reflect on all areas of your life and offer you the opportunity to make an honest assessment of what you need to change, enhance, balance or reduce whatever is required at any given time so that you can create the right flow of positive and negative energy to support you in the most powerful way possible.

One of the biggest tips I want to share with you is that you should be very aware that everything you do from this point onwards will have an impact on you in capacity, so it's really important to be conscious that just as positive chi can be created, negative chi can also be caused by chaos, clutter, people, your attitude and stressful environments. As Tony Robbins quotes;

"Where focus goes, energy flows…"

It's a great quote and SO TRUE. Whatever we focus our efforts on is what we are going to create more of, fact. This doesn't just mean your big goals for success with money, strong relationships or a multi-million-dollar business. It can also mean that if you spend all of your time obsessing or worrying about something that didn't work, someone who has frustrated you or somehow you didn't have the outcome you wanted, well, guess what my friend? If you continue to focus on that 'something'… you give energy to it and tell your mind, your thoughts and your subconscious that thing, 'something', matters most and that is what you will manifest.

This is why you now need to be very intentional with what you focus your precious energy in to, because to get what you REALLY want out of life, you need to focus the right amount of energy into everything you do. Just by changing to this thought process and being aware of your focused energy, you can utilise this powerful technique to change your flow and intentionally focus positive energy on the goal or outcome you desire.

When you can learn how to activate, enhance and cure an area of your home or office, you can start a flow of energy through your body, mind and soul for more success in your business, health, relationships and personal growth. By focusing and harnessing your energy in this way, an improved flow of energy will positively position you to attract more of what you desire, and amazing things will happen.

To ensure that you get the best possible start with this, take a moment to look at your current reality so that you can learn from it, be aware of it and change it — because you can, it's as simple as making a choice.

Sometimes we get so caught up in 'busy' that we don't see the true cause of the problem. Taking the time to pause and reflect, to do a simple reality-check will help you gain clarity on what you need to change and how you can get the outcome you desire.

Take a moment to reflect, breathe and answer these questions honestly:

What are you focusing your energy on right now?

Who are you focusing your energy on right now?

Do you need to focus on your energy to get better results?

What is the one thing can you change today to CHANGE the flow of energy for the better? *Do that.*

THE FORGOTTEN SECRET

The ancient art of Feng Shui is a mysterious, magical, intriguing and ambiguous annotation. My interpretation of this traditional philosophy is that if you can optimise the positive energy flowing into your life and environment, you have the opportunity to bring good fortune to yourself, your home and all who dwell in it. Practised correctly, it will also naturally bring more balance, peace and harmony to your mind, body and soul.

It's important to recognise that Feng Shui is not a new concept, and in fact, dates back to the time of ancient masters who focused on the flow of energy (or 'chi' as the Chinese call it) to be the essential life force for which everything is formed.

From another historical perspective, there are five key elements which hold the secret to balance and successful completion of increased energy, abundance, harmony and flow, also known as the 'Five Elements Life Cycle'.

This philosophy comes out of Taoism *(pronounced dow-ism)* which forms the umbrella of Chinese medicine. Phrases such as 'in the flow' 'go with the flow' or 'I want to find my flow', that's all from the work of Taoism as this 'flow' comes from nature and nature is our teacher of these five elements in the flow of our cycle of life. This right here is the key to balance and successful completion.

Together we're going to use these energetic frequencies, colour and objects to activate the flow of chi (energy) and remove any stagnant chi throughout your home and workplace.

You have the ability to shape the way you are experiencing life, and by understanding how to leverage this ancient artform within you and around you, with its power and influence, this is the greatest tool I can give you.

Now it's your time to ensure that ancient tradition continues in these modern times and continues to have profound results.

I AM
ALWAYS
MOTIVATED
TO TAKE
ACTION

THE BENEFITS OF CREATIVE
FENG SHUI

The main benefit of choosing to use Creative Feng Shui as the tool to enhance and activate your lifestyle choices is that it provides you with the energy to tap into an endless source of personal power and fortune which can instantly affect every area of daily life in the deepest, most positive way. It is also often recommended by psychologists because of the benefits of organisation, productivity, focus, creativity and relaxation.

By harnessing the powerful way energy within you blends with the energy around you, you can begin to make adjustments to the way you feel. The aim is to be able to intuitively self-scan and identify what needs changing so that you are more successful in everything that you do.

I know this may sound crazy and idealistic to some, but I truly believe that we are on the brink of an explosion of more types of energy medicine being available to us. With our intuitive intelligence needing to be developed as our hospitals and care centres are becoming more and more overstretched with viruses and disease, I envisage a changing world and future where energy healers and light-workers will be entrusted to scan our bodies for the lack of balance and deficiencies without invasive surgery or prescription drugs. With the right help, support and education, we will be able to detect imbalance within and have the knowledge to take the appropriate steps to help ourselves more intuitively.

This same self-scan can then be applied to our homes to create more harmony, serenity, balance, safety and calm as these simple energy techniques will enable you to create the ambience you need in your home. Working with the energy of yourself and your home allows you to protect, enhance or improve yourself and your space with an invisible force field.

In a well-received article in Forbes, Jamie Gold wrote;

"Creating an environmental sanctuary for the body to rest, relax and restore allows the limbic system to reset, as well as the parasympathetic and sympathetic nervous system to become balanced. Stress can cause the body to produce an excess amount of epinephrine (adrenaline), which then causes a weakening of the immune system," she explains:

"The benefits of feeling safe and comfortable with a positive mindset about the environment may lower chronic stress, which can lead to better blood sugar balance, stronger immune system, lower depression and anxiety. Because stress can weaken the immune system, most design principles that minimize stress have a positive impact on the immune system. This is important because the impairment of the immune system can make people more vulnerable to various diseases, including, some scientists argue, cancer." the physician notes.

I am not for one second saying that Creative Feng Shui or any energy work for that matter is a cure for major illnesses and disease, my thoughts are based on simply being able to help ourselves learn about our intuition as our bodies and the body of our home constantly sends messages. We just need to learn how to understand what we're being told a little better and then maybe, just maybe, we could help ourselves more and more.

The art of being able to do more of this is realising that if you desire something like 'greater confidence' in order to succeed more in your business, you can use Creative Feng Shui as the tool to enhance this characteristic **within yourself**.

What you shouldn't do is assume that Creative Feng Shui will magically make your business more successful just because you wrote an intention. It's all within you, and the focused, purposeful, intentional action you take to make your intentions and goals become a reality.

With this in mind, you can apply Creative Feng Shui to any aspect of your life or environment which you can have a direct influence on. For example, if you would like to create more relationships with key individuals, you might need to become more visible; to get quicker client conversions, you might need to become more assertive; and to have an improved love life, you might need to show better compassion.

What Creative Feng Shui cannot help with are events out of your sphere of influence. So, it is unlikely that money will flow in from nowhere or that the perfect partner will arrive out of the blue. You have to be aware of what you can and cannot control.

The benefit of Creative Feng Shi is that it can be applied to everything within your life and environment. This includes your health, moods, emotions, relationships, creativity, family life, business, career development, travel, the ability to manage and grow your finances and your plans for the future.

When you decide to take intentional action on making your home and workspace feel and look better, it instantly activates the sense of feeling stronger, happier and healthier. The added advantage of using Creative Feng Shui as your tool to benefit from this allows you to strategically influence these interactions to achieve specific life improvements by positioning yourself and your surroundings in aligned harmony with principles of natural energy flow. As a result, you can achieve more balance with everything you're surrounded by.

In addition to the benefits I've already shared, Creative Feng Shui can also help:

IMPROVE YOUR LOVING RELATIONSHIPS

Every kind of relationship can be improved through effective enhancements with Creative Feng Shui. Whether you are a single person attracting love, enhancing an already existing relationship, or *improving* your *relationship* with your children. You can activate love, harmony and happiness if this is what you desire.

ATTRACT MORE FINANCIAL WEALTH

The Creative Feng Shui approach to wealth helps make way for all the riches, money and wealth to find you easily and effortlessly by balancing the energies in a home or office to enhance the inflow of money and dramatically reduce the outflow – or unnecessary, unwanted and unexpected outflow of it.

DEVELOP YOUR FAME & NOTORIETY

Creative Feng Shui can enhance your endeavours toward building a favourable impression, reputation or standing with everyone you encounter. Then your fame's impact will be recognised and help position you for success with more people and opportunities.

ADVANCE YOUR CAREER

Associated not only with a job, career or business, Creative Feng Shui helps you connect with your personal genius so that you can broaden your vision for your life's path, explore potential opportunities and discover and follow your deepest passion.

INCREASE YOUR CREATIVITY

Even if you don't consider yourself creative, we all have some way we use this influence in our lives. Creative Feng Shui activates the energy of creation and successful completion of anything you create or birth into the world.

PROMOTE YOUR PHYSICAL WELLBEING

By utilizing Creative Feng Shui to bring good chi to your health and wellbeing, it can improve your health on a physical, mental, emotional, and spiritual level, as well as promote peace and harmony in your family.

EXPAND YOUR PERSONAL GROWTH

Creative Feng Shui helps you assimilate new information with a clear and open mind, and it helps you make choices that benefit your life.

PROTECT YOUR ENERGY

Just as Creative Feng Shui can increase good energy, it can also help avoid negative energies that can cause bad luck, confrontation, stress and harm.

RAISE YOUR VIBRATION

When the energies in our space harmonise with our own chi, we are more frequently in tune with the universal flow of energy which naturally raises our own vibrations so that we can align to our true selves and unlock our full potential.

In order to live an optimal life, you must have optimal surroundings. Creative Feng Shui will provide you with a set of principles that you can apply to your surroundings in order to experience greater pleasure, fulfilment and satisfaction in whatever it is that you're doing. It's also a wonderful way to bring a consciousness to everything within your environment. In other words, you will naturally become more mindful when you fully apply this philosophy.

When your environment feels nurturing and supportive, you're better able to relax and concentrate on what you're trying to accomplish. Whether it's working, resting or socialising with friends. This way of living helps you experience your everyday surroundings in new, more meaningful ways.

I AM
POSITIVE
&
OPTIMISTIC

PREPARE TO WORK YOUR MAGIC

CREATE SPACE

It's essential that before we start making significant changes in every area of your life, we need to make space - both internally and externally – for you to really feel and see Creative Feng Shui work its magic.

If there is one thing you can do right now which will make a huge difference to your life, home and business, it's to create space. Physical space, mental space and emotional space.

Never before has the need for space been so prevalent. Our world and environment have shifted so much that we are physically losing space to live, be free, breathe and re-energise. So many things demand our attention, time and energy that we don't even realise how little space we have until we start creating more of it.

Without space, your hopes and dreams don't have room to breathe, your creativity and flow may be stifled, and you can easily feel overwhelmed. Not only is it the essential component of inspired work, but it also provides you with the opportunity to gain more clarity and be able to reflect, assess, make improvements and change what's not working for you.

This doesn't mean that you have to overhaul your entire life, get rid of everything and turn your home upside down, but it does mean becoming aware of negative energy so that we can start making improvements, today.

To make space is to structure your life in a way that you can give your life, your business and your home space to breathe and grow so that you can set yourself up for success in everything you do and everywhere you are.

Our aim here is to turn negative space into a positive outcome, so I recommend starting where all the negative energy shows up most, it's relentless in its efforts to hold you back, create chaos and block you at every stage – *your mind.*

Being able to detach from drama, embrace the good and show yourself more compassion will help you gain more focus on what you really want to achieve with intention and gratitude.

A cluttered mind is restless and unfocused. It tries to move in lots of different directions all at the same time and only ever results in getting very little done. If you're worrying about the future, reminiscing about the past, keeping a mental to-do list, complaining about that 'something', you're applying an awful lot of negative brain energy to fear-based thinking without even realising.

Clearing space in your mind allows you to be conscious of your thoughts, be open to change and helps refocus the energy of feeling negative, stuck, unproductive and unhealthy into more positive thoughts and actions.

Fortunately, there are strategies and techniques you can use to clean out some space in your head. Here's what I recommend:

WRITE IT DOWN

You don't need to keep everything stored in your brain. There's so much power putting pen to paper. I encourage you to carry a notebook and pen so that you always have a way to 'brain dump' what's on your mind and completely empty your head onto those pages. This can include appointments you need to make, social media posts, ideas for future projects, and so on.

KEEP A JOURNAL

Keeping a journal is similar to the previous point, 'write it down', but with more depth, meaning and thoughts of how you're feeling. A journal allows you to download the inner chatter that's constantly interrupting your thought process when you're trying to get important tasks done. For example, you can write in your journal:

- Things that you're worried about
- Plans for achieving an important goal
- Concerns about a relationship that's draining your energy
- What's going on in your life right now
- Who and what you're grateful for
- Your dreams for the future

Writing down your thoughts can be extremely cathartic. It can also have an amazing effect when you're acknowledging its importance and releasing it to the universe for forgiveness, gratitude, hope, love and anything you wish to manifest.

LET GO OF THE PAST

Mind clutter is often related to the past. Mistakes you've made, opportunities you've missed, people you've hurt, things that didn't work, grievances – it's time to discard memories of the past that are no longer serving you and are just draining the energy from your current life and future possibilities. *Let it go.*

STOP MULTI-TASKING

If your house is a mess and you need to organise and declutter it, how would you begin? I'm hoping that by the time you've read this book that you would start by choosing one important area, for example, the desk in your office and clear it of all unnecessary clutter.

The mental equivalent of clearing off your desk is to allocate a certain amount of time to which you're going to devote exclusively to one important task.

During that timeframe, push all mental clutter aside and focus all of your attention and energy on the task at hand. Visualise your desk that is clear of everything other than that **one task** which you're going to be working on. Make sure that your desk stays completely clear of all other items during the entire chunk of time that you've devoted to this task. If anything else tries to work its way onto the table or into your ear, mentally push it away until you have completed what you set out to do.

GROUND YOURSELF

Meditation, mantras, intuitive alignment and positive affirmations make great tools to make this happen, as they provide the opportunity to ground ourselves, reduce stress and enhance the feeling of calm.

AND BREATHE...

It's amazing how much space just one deep breath can create. Make it three; one to calm the body, one to collect your thoughts, and one to set an intention. Take three spacious moments to take a deep inhale and a heavy realising sigh out breath each time. Do this on the hour, every hour to create an abundance of headspace throughout your day. *It really does feel amazing...*

Just think of all the clarity that you'll have with your decision-making and how your creativity, intuition or focus will thrive without the busy chitter-chatter of mental chaos.

CLEAR THE CLUTTER

The reason why we focus on clearing up our mind, the body of our home and the heart and soul of our life before we apply the Creative Feng Shui technique is because clutter creates stagnant energy, drains any positive energy you may have and dampens your best intentions.

Every aspect of your life is anchored energetically into your living space, so clearing your clutter can completely transform your entire existence, whilst also making space for the new energy and opportunities to arrive.

Going forward, Creative Feng Shui will become your go-to energy tool for helping you clear your clutter in the most efficient and enjoyable way. But first, we need to try to get the best possible start so that you see the results start to happen before your very eyes.

As a self-confessed recovering hoarder, I want to re-assure you that this isn't about perfection, it's about inspired action and being open to making more space by removing items and obstacles which no longer serve you or you don't need.

We are constantly bombarded by marketing messages and promotions that make it too hard for us *not* to buy. We end up buying lots of 'things' that will end up gathering dust, *(sometimes unused)* somewhere in our home, and we don't want to throw anything away because we *might use it someday*. Notice the royal 'we' here?

Clutter makes you waste time and money as you will inevitably spend a considerable amount of time looking for your stuff. You may even buy duplicates of the same item because you either can't find what you're looking for or you've forgotten that you had it already.

It's also possible to create social problems by not keeping your space free from clutter because when your house is in chaos, you're less likely to invite guests over as you feel embarrassed and self-conscious by the mess you've created which then manifests more stress, panic and feeling helpless in making improvements.

All of this, from personal experience, translates to a lower quality of living. Over time, these problems can escalate to the point where your life seems blocked. Perhaps many people have this sort of problem, hence the popularity of decluttering, which is a whole other book in itself.

One of the most important steps of good feng shui is to get rid of everything you do not love in your house. Clutter clearing will help you 'lighten up the load', and it is essential for harmonious living. Here's what you can do to instantly change the energy of your space:

CLEAR CLUTTER FROM SPACES THAT GREET YOU WHEN YOU FIRST ENTER YOUR HOME.

The condition of the space that greets you when you first enter your home has an immediate effect on your energy. If it's neat, smells nice, looks organised, feels clean and oozes loveliness, you will feel comforted and your energy is likely to significantly improve.

If, however, you are greeted by a chaotic environment with lots of clutter, dust, dirt and grime, your energy will feel depleted and trapped because you are being bombarded by the negative energy of the space. Create a clutter free greeting, and everything that happens after you enter your home is likely to be more peaceful and positive.

CLEAR CLUTTER FROM SPACES WHERE YOU SPEND THE MOST TIME.

After you create a positive greeting, you can move on to clearing the clutter in your office, kitchen and family room, places where you spend significant amounts of time. The energy where you spend the most time has the most impact on your overall energy so by clearing your clutter, helps change the stagnant energies of those spaces from negative to positive. This positive energy then results in positive interactions with others, positive experiences, and optimal productivity.

CLEAR CLUTTER FROM YOUR BEDROOM.

You spend more time sleeping than doing any other activity in your home. The quality of your sleep is directly affected by the condition of your bedroom. A cluttered bedroom is full of negative energy. Negative energy is noisy energy, alerting you to the fact that all is not well, that there are things that need to be done. It's hard to sleep well when distracted by the shouting chorus of bedroom clutter. And, persistent clutter in the bedroom can have a profound impact on health because you are being exposed to that negative energy for prolonged periods of time.

CLEAR OUT ANYTHING THAT IS BROKEN THAT CAN'T BE QUICKLY FIXED OR THAT IS NOT WORTH FIXING.

Broken things attract being broke or having a broken body (health issues). They are strong sources of negative energy requiring some type of work on your part. If you accumulate a collection of broken items, you are likely to start to feel broken. Decide quickly whether a broken item is worth the effort and/or cost necessary to fix it. If fixing it is not worth doing, ditch it quickly. If it is worth fixing, take immediate steps to fix it.

I AM
COURAGEOUS

GET INTENTIONAL

The power of thought is one of the strongest and most useful powers you possess. Together with your imagination, creativity and intention, you can create success or failure, happiness or unhappiness, opportunities or obstacles. You're in the driver's seat.

We have the ability to choose our realities and manifest our desires through intention, belief, focus, inspired action and commitment. If you believe that our minds can create our realities, then the concept of Creative Feng Shui will be a game-changer for you.

Creative Feng Shui teaches the power of intention. By getting clear about what you intend to do, you make a commitment to yourself to do it. Setting your intentions is about understanding what you're doing, why you're doing it, and how you're going to do it.

When you make a choice to live and work with intention, everything changes. You have everything you need to pursue what matters most. You are not at the mercy of trends or what is happening anywhere else, you are consciously creating the life you want to live, and it's transformative because you can actively create the extraordinary.

There is an energy that when you harness it, it can elevate and propel your life beyond what you thought imaginable. You, my friend, are the master of your own destiny and I hope you're excited about getting a whole lot more intentional about what's possible.

Michael Simmons, who has studied the lives of Oprah Winfrey, Albert Einstein and Warren Buffett, among others writes; 'Despite having way more responsibility than anyone else, top performers in the business world often find time to step away from their urgent work, slow down, and invest in activities that have a long-term payoff in greater knowledge, creativity, and energy,' so it's also a well-known fact that top executives, innovators and 'successful people' set intentions and live intentionally.

Intention setting utilises dormant energy and directs it towards a particular outcome. This can be as simple as determining a clear goal at the beginning of each small task or activity, visioning yourself at the start completing it successfully with the intended outcomes you desire.

Our thoughts are powerful. The power of intention is an integral part of our ability to achieve our goals. If there is intention behind all that we accomplish and by applying conscious intention, the effectiveness is improved greatly.

BUT WHAT IS AN INTENTION?

An intention is the purest form of your goal; it's the essence of your goal. Intention is the heart of your deepest desire, wants, ideas, and creativity. Intentions set the foundation for our goal, and from that place of intention, we can build a plan of action to achieve our goal.

When we set an intention of how we want to feel, act, and show up as we move through our life, your goal is one particular manifestation of your deep intention.

I believe that setting an intention sows a seed that sparks a mighty mindset shift that has the power to make a dramatic change. You should 'set your intention' when you aim for positive change in particular areas of your life, without pre-determining the outcome you desire.

It is very important that you not define too closely the result you think you want. Part of the power of intention is that it brings you into a place you might not have expected, but that opens up new pathways to growth and happiness in your life.

Here's how we'll set intentions with the core principles of Creative Feng Shui:

Step 1. Choose what area of your life you want to focus your intention. An intention embodies the feeling you would like to cultivate in your life. Often intentions begin with themes around love, trust, connection, wisdom, health and money. Think big picture personalised to you as an individual, without limits or constraints of time or earning potential.

Step 2. Explore the purpose of the intention. Why you are doing something is just as important as what you are doing because it generates more meaning. Knowing your why helps you define your purpose. How will your intention serve you? How does the intention benefit your life as a whole? Knowing your why is a powerful motivator.

Step 3. Visualise the how you'd like to feel or what you would like to achieve and put pen to paper starting with 'I AM' and ending with 'and more' where possible. Place them in your success areas and check-in on them every day.

Step 4. Trust the process.

The secret to success here is letting go of some of the control and trusting that your heart and intuition can be your guide. This is the foundation of powerful intention setting. It's also the key ingredient to living a life of fulfilment. What do you hope to manifest in your life? Give intention setting a try.

YOUR MAGIC MAP

Before you start out on any adventure, it's always advisable to have a map and a guide to assure you that you are heading in the right direction. The methodology of Creative Feng Shui is to use the traditional principles of the 'Bagua Map' grid approach as the foundation for your energy to start flowing through your space.

The 'Bagua Map' looks like this:

WEALTH & ABUNDANCE	FAME & REPUTATION	LOVE & RELATIONSHIPS
FAMILY & NEW BEGINNINGS	HEALTH & CENTERING	CREATIVITY & LEGACY
WISDOM & KNOWLEDGE	CAREER & LIFE JOURNEY	TRAVEL & HELPFUL PEOPLE

YOUR FRONT DOOR

We will use this grid style map as a starting point to locate and activate a positive flow of energy, wherever you would like to create it. This works for the layout of your desk, office, living space and whole environment.

You can start using this instantly by simply standing outside your door looking inwards as that's exactly where your positive energy will start flowing in from. The best way to utilise this is to create a floorplan of your space and draw the above grid system over the top (ensuring that your front door is aligned with the bottom part of the grid), you can then see where these directions are located.

As a general guide, the back-left part of your home is associated with wealth & abundance, the back-middle is associated with recognition & how you are perceived, the back-left associated with love & relationships and you can use the grid above to match in the remaining areas.

The 'Bagua Map' is considered an essential tool for transforming your home and is an energy map of your space which is often referred to as 'The Magic Map'. Through the practice of Creative Feng Shui, your ability to recognise subtle energy shifts and vibrations around you will be heightened and using the Bagua Map, you will be able to form a connection between your inner intuition and outer world.

Have you ever walked into a home that feels welcoming, like a warm hug that you never want to leave? Whilst in other homes, you have felt this heavy and negative energy hit your gut, causing alarm bells and a desire to run? This is your subconscious mind communicating with you, and letting you know if something is good or bad. Start to really pay attention to these feelings, notice how situations, environments or people make you feel because your intuition is rarely wrong. This will serve you in all areas of your life.

THE 'LIFE CYCLE'

In addition to the 'Bagua Map,' Creative Feng Shui further enhances this powerful energy portal with your personal energy archetype, directions of a compass, elements of nature, quantum colours and numerology for the ultimate opportunity to stimulate an abundance of positive flow of chi, quickly and effortlessly.

This is called the 'Life Cycle Wheel' as it's basically your wheel of life which moves, positions and directs you in the right direction for optimal success for everything you desire. The 'Life Cycle Wheel' will also be used to create your personalised vision board later in the book.

The 'Life Cycle Wheel' looks like this:

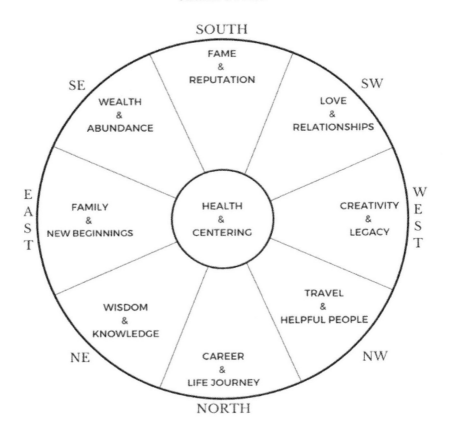

To avoid any confusion at this point, remember that the 'Bagua Map' lays the foundation for energy to start flowing within your overall space, from your front door. The 'Life Cycle Wheel' then allows you to layer, apply and work in conjunction with your own personal energy number activations and enhancements based on your more fortunate directions.

This combination, when utilised together, will become the secret formula for your environment and used to enhance the energy flow to your intentional living desires.

KNOW YOUR NUMBERS

Did you know that your date of birth associates you with one of the numbers 1-9 in Creative Feng Shui? Your birth date gives you a unique number that says a lot about who you are and how you can best nourish yourself in your space. Knowing your Feng Shui number gives you another way to bring balance and harmony into your life.

Numbers and numerology are at the heart of Creative Feng Shui as they are the components that provide clues to how the cosmic vibrations in our living environments interact with our inner vibrations. Numbers, and the way they combine with each other, reveal influences that have a direct impact on the kind of people we eventually become and help translate the meaning of messages which we are constantly receiving.

Mathematicians view numbers as the universal language. But numerologists believe the numbers in your life can determine who you are and what you can do. When you study the meanings associated with your birth numbers (your personal energy number), you will get a very good feel about your character tendencies, how you respond to others and to the events in your life.

Numerology is the practice of reading and acting on the meanings of numbers as well as their sums and combinations. The sum of the numbers associated with our birthday for this instance, tells us a great deal about our aptitudes and character tendencies.

It is an excellent way of tapping into strengths that energise you the most, whilst also acting as an introduction to your personality, what makes you tick, what gets you excited, and by natural extension, what aspirations you have.

Learning the significance of your birth number (we'll refer to this going forward as your personal energy number), is believed to be the most significant of the main numbers in numerology and Creative Feng Shui. It reveals the potential in your life and has the most fortunate energy flow naturally attached to it.

Your personal energy number suggests what will bring you the greatest potential for success, alignment, fulfilment, flow and happiness. Knowing your number is the beginning of a journey into understanding your inner magnetism and allows you to tap into your individual directions to create more success, wealth, health, and love in your life.

You can instantly access your personal energy number by visiting: https://www.sarahstone.com/personal-energy-number or you can work it out manually using the formula below.

Before we do anything further, it's important to know:

- The personal energy number calculations for a female are different from the personal energy number calculations.

READY TO KNOW YOUR NUMBER?

Before we do anything further, it's important to know:

- The personal energy number calculations for a female are different from the personal energy number calculations for a male. Don't worry though, I'll provide you with an example for both.

- For those born after the year 2000, the personal energy number calculations are slightly different.

PERSONAL ENERGY NUMBER FOR A FEMALE
(born before the year 2000):

Basically, each number is added together until it's reduced to a single digit. Some numbers require multiple reductions to achieve this. Keep repeating the calculation until you reach a single digit.

Let's use the birth date of April 8, 1979 as an example:

Add the last two digits of the year of birth: 7 + 9 = 16
Bring it to a single digit number: 1 + 6 = 7
Add your single digit number to number 5: 7 + 5 = 12

Bring it to a single digit number: 1 + 2 = 3
The single digit is your personal energy
number: 3

NOTE: For a female born after the year 2000, add the number 6 instead of 5.

PERSONAL ENERGY NUMBER FOR A MALE *(born before the year 2000):*

Basically, each number is added together until it's reduced to a single digit. Some numbers require multiple reductions to achieve this. Keep repeating the calculation until you reach a single digit.

Let's use the birth date of April 23, 1977 as an example:

Add the last two digits of the year of birth: 7 +
7 = 14
Bring it to a single digit number: 1 + 4 = 5
Deduct the single digit number from 10: 10 − 5 = 5
The single digit is your personal energy
number: 5

NOTE: For a male born after the year 2000, deduct from 9 instead of 10. Also, a male born in 2009 and 2018 will have the Personal Energy Number 9.

I AM
THE PERSON
I WAS
MEANT TO
BECOME

EXPLORING PERSONAL ENERGY ARCHETYPES

You probably have heard about archetypes more than once in your life, referring to different types of people, their characteristics and tendencies based on specific questions or situations.

Archetypes of the five elements and your personal energy number are at the root of the Creative Feng Shui life areas, and the way they combine with each other to help you tune in to your own inner insight.

The meaning and symbolism of the magic numbers from 1-9 represents an energy number archetype which represents a particular type of energy suggested by the Five Elements of Creative Feng Shui. Discover what your personal energy number archetype says about you...

NUMBER 1 – THE CREATOR

Nature Element: Water
Season: Winter
Trait: Independent
Quantum Colours: Black and Blue
Your Power Directions: South East, East, South, North

Personality Characteristics: *Creator of fortune, wealth, opportunities and legacy. Sociable, diplomatic makes connections easily, independent, intuitive and a good listener. A leader, explorer, writer.*

I n your archetype of 'The Creator' your dominant element Water. You are beautifully intuitive, flexible and adaptable in your approach to life and business. You have the innate ability to create an abundance of wealth and prosperity for yourself and those you love. Your excellent communication skills support you in making valuable negotiations as well as enhancing your ability to build positive relationships that reflect your empathic ear, supportive nature and nurturing qualities you share with everyone you meet. With a holistic view to life, you portray artistic, sociable, diplomatic and creative personality traits which allow you to touch everyone's heart.

You are a natural-born leader and thrive independently with your powerful connection to your intuition, which you can call on in any given moment. You are likely to be pursuing a career path that is creative in nature, such as writing, publishing, and finding fortune in everything you do. The element of water itself symbolises winter, and water can be symbolised in your personality as gentle rain or a storm.

You do need to be aware of not becoming too sensitive, fickle and intrusive to others as this can enhance and stimulate the feelings of fear, nervousness and stress. Therefore, spending more time with your family will bring you inner peace and enhance your self-esteem.

NUMBER 2 – THE EDUCATOR

Nature Element: Earth
Season: Summer into Autumn
Trait: Methodical
Quantum Colours: Yellow, Orange and Earth Tones
Your Power Directions: North East, West, North West, South West

---

Personality Characteristics: Awe-inspiring and compelled to share their wisdom and knowledge with the world. The master of their destiny. Methodical, supportive, helpful, reliable and nurturing. Fair and patient, works well within groups, a stabilising force, can be overly fussy. Diplomat, teacher, organiser, service professional.

I n your archetype of 'The Educator' your dominant element is Earth. You are the safe haven and rock for all of those that are fortunate enough to meet you. Your supportive and down to earth nature attracts people to you like a moth to a flame as you continue to provide stability and assurance that is often lacking in the world of others.

You possess such inner strength and positivity that you continue to be the voice of reason in any crisis. However, be careful not to get embroiled in the chaos. This makes you an excellent team player who can act as the grounding force for others. You don't like to rush anything and continue to provide patience, care, compassion, reliability, and nurturing support to those around you. You are the ideal Chi for improving the quality of whatever you do.

You value loyalty and cannot be faulted for your patience and compassion towards others. This allows you to create great relationships that reflect your qualities of being supportive, helpful, reliable and professional. Your career path is likely to reflect that of a teacher, mentor, community leader, organiser, or supportive professional and you take pride in all that you do which can often lead to perfectionism and being overly fussy.

NUMBER 3 – THE ILLUMINATOR

Nature Element: Wood
Season: Spring
Trait: Progressive
Quantum Colours: Green tones
**Your Power Directions: South, North, South
East, East**

Personality Characteristics: *Passionate, enthusiastic, fiercely loyal, trustworthy, dedicated, fully invested, energised, persistent, hardworking and creative. With an eye for detail, looks at the world with a fresh perspective enabling others to capitalise on opportunities.*

In your archetype of 'The Illuminator,' your dominant element is wood. You are an energetic, enthusiastic, artistic soul who undertakes all tasks with an unwavering passion. You thrive off helping share the light of others which wins you loyal support and friendship.

As an ideas person, your brain is programmed to see a world of opportunity and vision that can change the world, however, you possess a trait of rather than committing to a plan, you sometimes fail to bring your vision to fruition as you prioritise others over yourself.

You gain reward and fulfilment from encouraging enthusiasm, positive outcomes and instilling self-esteem. You are quietly confident and can be assertive when the need requires. You have the desire to start new innovative projects and like to focus on details, be extremely precise, get the best results, but you also require dedicated time, space to concentrate and be able to analyse your work.

You are driven to succeed yet can become disheartened when your contribution isn't valued or appreciated.

Nourishment is key for the Illuminator. You should regularly re-energise and create balance in your life by spending time outdoors in nature with loved ones and friends.

NUMBER 4 – THE STRATEGIST

**Nature Element: Wood
Season: Spring into Summer
Trait: Adaptable
Quantum Colours: Green / Blue
Your Power Directions: North, South, East,
South East**

Personality Characteristics: *Versatile, decisive and adaptable. An independent perfectionist, realist and natural networker. An idea's person with a keen eye for detail and ability to bring forth an action plan that is implemented with lightning speed.*

I n your archetype of 'The Strategist,' your dominant element is Wood. Rising to every task in your pursuit of cultivating ideas and strategies. Not one to hold back from rising to the task at hand, they are brilliant at conceptualizing their ideas, mobilizing resources and executing the action plan to achieve their goals.

You are a trailblazer with an exact vision of your future and are relentless in making un-wavering progress in your life improvement and continually working on future prosperity.

You flourish and thrive in an environment that allows you full scope to bring forth your ideas. You prefer to work alone, but you must not forget to include others in your journey of change.

Your make-up is designed to keep them alert, focus on details, get things right, analyse, be precise, but they need space to concentrate. You enjoy learning about wealth and the process of creating prosperity and this motivates you to share this strategy of abundance with others.

Your energy needs regular time in nature and sunshine to recharge and replenish. This will be where you are more likely to tap into your intuition, download your best ideas and create a constant source of happiness for yourself and your family.

NUMBER 5 (FEMALE) – THE CONSCIOUS NURTURER

Nature Element: Earth, Central Force
Season: Late Summer
Trait: Intuitive
Quantum Colours:
Power Directions: South West, North West, West, North East

Personality Characteristics: *One of a kind, heart centred, highly intuitive, compassionate, affectionate, and generous. Craves deep, meaningful relationships where they can have open and honest communications. Quick minded, resilient and instinctive.*

I n your archetype of 'The Conscious Nurturer,' your dominant element is the central force of Earth. Drawing upon the qualities of all the other archetypes, it is easy for you to find yourself in the centre holding a safe space of nurture for others, however, it´s important that you don´t lose yourself in the process.

As a highly intuitive empath, you are sensitive to the needs of others, remember to ground yourself as the individualised process of prescriptive support can drain your energy. You treat everyone you meet as an equal, accepting and offering a space of non-judgemental advice and support.

Like mother Earth, you offer constant nourishment for others but understand this, in order for you to fully thrive you need to understand and be aware of how to replenish & re-energise, for you to consistently give yourself to others. You have a calm and tranquil nature that is consistent unless threatened, un-recognised or taken for granted.

Good exercise is paramount. Meditation, yoga, qi gong, or anything else that involves movement and flow will revive your energy and is your natural path for growth.

Your greatest wisdom and success will come from connecting to the centre of your world through heart-centred relationships, networks, collaborations and love focused contribution.

Nature Element: Earth
Season: Summer into Autumn
Trait: Methodical
Quantum Colours: Yellow, Orange and Earth Tones
Your Power Directions: North East, West, North West, South West

---

Personality Characteristics: *Knowledgeable, educated, practical, wise, thorough, decisive, teacher, well organised, philosopher, teacher, author, here to leave a legacy and be a mentor to others.*

In your archetype of 'The Instructor,' your dominant element is Earth. You live life with integrity and have traits of a true leader.

Sharing your well researched knowledge with care, you offer great insight and share your wisdom which instils confidence in others. The earth element is helpful for deepening all kinds of relationships.

Supportive and loyal, you are a tower of strength and lead others in the right direction.

You have a personal quest to always seek the truth, meaning that you have strong beliefs which can be unforgiving, blunt and detached, which can lead to becoming suspicious and passive of others.

To revitalise your energy, ground yourself in nature. Practice regular movement, time to stop, allow, breathe the fresh air, recharge and replenish is essential for you. This will be where you are more likely to get your best perils of wisdom.

NUMBER 6 – THE CREATIVE THINKER

Nature Element: Metal
Season: Autumn into Winter
Trait: Relentless
Quantum Colours: Silver / Grey / White
Power Directions: West, North East, South West, North West

Personality Characteristics: *Driven, innovative, lateral thinker, open minded, adapts well to change. Strong communicator, open minded, creative thinker and innovative with a finger on the pulse.*

In your archetype of 'The Creative Thinker,' your dominant element is Metal. As a creator of breakthrough ideas, you have a natural tendency towards lateral thinking, developing novel or unorthodox approaches to solving problems. Critical thinking comes easily to you, as does analysing and communicating the multi-faceted opportunities that you create.

Bringing a fresh perspective to life and all that you do, you will often create more efficient ways of doing things, with an independence and single mindedness that can be off putting to others. You can sometimes be perceived as being inflexible and serious and do not necessarily accept help from others easily.

Good for being in charge, dignified and responsible, you have an increased desire to organise, plan ahead, be respected and have integrity. This represents experience and maturity, finding it easy to win people's trust.

Metal personalities are magnanimous and resolute, pursuing their ambitions with great strength, consistency and high standards. Your greatest inspirations will come from being more playful and fluid, providing you with greater wisdom and clearer intuition.

NUMBER 7 – THE INTUITIVE LEADER

Nature Element: Metal
Season: Autumn
Trait: Flexible
Quantum Colours: Rusty Reds / Maroon / Pink
Power Directions: North West, South West, North East, West

Personality Characteristics: *Innate wisdom, well organised, perfectionist, consistent, authoritative, confident, well organised, efficient, respectful, interesting, intuitive and instinctive.*

In your archetype of 'The Intuitive Leader,' your dominant element is Metal. A natural born leader and greater communicator, you have a strong sense about people, can anticipate trends and move with great confidence through any challenge you are faced with.

You possess the natural ability to act with integrity and take charge of situations in a dignified and responsible manner. It's your mission to find a solution for the highest good of all, which makes it easy for you to earn people's trust, admiration and respect.

Metal personalities are magnanimous and resolute. You are extremely consistent and methodical within your approach and have a tendency to take things a little too seriously. Don't be afraid to relax, let your hair down more and embrace the fun side of your personality.

Replenish your soul by nurturing yourself, spending time surrounded by children having fun and being inspired by things which bring you joy. The support of your family and friends are crucial to your future success.

NUMBER 8 – THE CONFIDANTE

Nature Element: Earth
Season: Winter into Spring
Trait: Patient
Quantum Colours:
Power Directions: North East, North West, West,
North East

Personality Characteristics: *Patient, kind, compassionate, fair, practical, down to earth, supportive collaborator, helpful, composed, trusted, loyal, reliable and nurturing personality.*

I n your archetype of 'The Confidante,' your dominant element is Earth. You are a down-to-earth, caring, fair, patient and a compassionate listener who people often share their innermost secrets with.

As a natural caretaker, your 'Mother Earth' nurturing qualities lends itself to connecting and collaborating with others and support your desire to bring more life to the world and provide others with more physical, mental and spiritual sustenance.

You are responsible, protective, loving, loyal and compassionate but you run the risk of prioritising other people over yourself, which often means that you are constantly neglecting your own needs and finding it difficult to establish boundaries in life and business.

Your maternal persistence enhances your character to take action, but be aware that this also means that you have a tendency to be stubborn and have difficulty 'letting go' of things outside of your control.

Take time for meditation, intuitive alignment and breath work as this will help clear your mind, nourish your growth and stimulate your vitality.

NUMBER 9 – THE ALCHEMIST

Nature Element: Fire
Season: Summer
Trait: Impulsive
Quantum Colours: Red / Purple
Power Directions: East, South East, North, South

Personality Characteristics: *Clarity of vision, risk-taker, passionate, inspirational, excellent communicators, passionate, outgoing, sociable, proud, honourable, and has great attention to detail.*

In your archetype of 'The Alchemist' your dominant element is Fire. You are able to work your magical intelligence on the world and are an agent of change.

Your fiery energy shines bright. Oozing enthusiasm, motivation and excitement for everything you do and everyone you surround yourself with. People are drawn to your charm and passion for life.

A challenge you face is where to focus your energy, but when you do, you can manifest anything you want. You are a bundle of magnetic energy, however, even you have your limits. Dispersing your energy in too many directions will deplete your vitality which means in extreme cases, you could burn out and become depressed.

Learning to say no to protect your energy will allow you to make space for new possibilities and perspective. To re-ignite your passion for life and business, spend time connecting, enjoying the company of friends, listen to music and dance will inspire your soul.

Did you get any **AHA!** moments when reading about the archetypes and the life areas? You can find out more about your personal archetype at: www.sarahstone.com/archetypes.

I AM
LEARNING
TO TRUST
THE PROCESS

SEEK YOUR BEST DIRECTIONS

Now that you know your personal energy number, have an understanding of your archetype and what it means, a whole new world will open up to you! Once you know your personal energy number, you can easily find out your more fortunate directions and use it in complete alignment with the 'Life Cycle Wheel':

PERSONAL ENERGY NUMBER	SUCCESS & MONEY FLOW	HEALTH & VITALITY	PERSONAL & PROFESSIONAL RELATIONSHIPS	PERSONAL GROWTH
1	SOUTH EAST	EAST	SOUTH	NORTH
2	NORTH EAST	WEST	NORTH WEST	SOUTH WEST
3	SOUTH	NORTH	SOUTH EAST	EAST
4	NORTH	SOUTH	EAST	SOUTH EAST
5 (FEMALE)	SOUTH WEST	NORTH WEST	WEST	NORTH EAST
5 (MALE)	NORTH EAST	WEST	NORTH WEST	SOUTH WEST
6	WEST	NORTH EAST	SOUTH WEST	NORTH WEST
7	NORTH WEST	SOUTH WEST	NORTH EAST	WEST
8	NORTH EAST	NORTH WEST	WEST	NORTH EAST
9	EAST	SOUTH EAST	NORTH	SOUTH

The methodology of these directions is simple; the meaning of more fortunate directions is that you receive better energies from some directions and inauspicious energies from other directions.

LOCATING YOUR LUCKY DIRECTIONS

Your lucky directions help you attract the quality of energy that is most nourishing, or suitable, for you personally. Once you know your lucky directions, you should then try to face them at work, at home, and when you sleep (the direction the crown of your head is facing when you are in bed).

To find your best directions, the easiest way to do this is to start at your front door. This is where your energy flows in from and it allows you to apply the foundational 'Bagua Map' grid as your starting point.

Note that by the "front door" in Creative Feng Shui, this means the actual front door that the house was built with, not the side door or the back door.

WEALTH & ABUNDANCE	FAME & REPUTATION	LOVE & RELATIONSHIPS
FAMILY & NEW BEGINNINGS	HEALTH & CENTERING	CREATIVITY & LEGACY
WISDOM & KNOWLEDGE	CAREER & LIFE JOURNEY	TRAVEL & HELPFUL PEOPLE

YOUR FRONT DOOR

When you are aware of the general directions and where the energy flows, you can then enhance your space even more by applying your personalised 'Life Cycle Wheel' to seek and find your optimal spaces by using a compass, your personal energy number and the best directions for your success & money flow, personal & professional relationships, health & vitality and personal growth.

Overlay and enhance your personal directions with the main Bagua grid and utilise the best of the combination of energy. For an additional explanation of how to utilise this further, I have created you a video tutorial which you can view over on the website at: www.sarahstone.com/ book-resources.

SOUTH - FAME, RECOGNITION & REPUTATION

Nature Element: Fire
Magic Number: 9
Season: Summer
Colour: Red / Purple

The South represents the luck of your success and recognition. In the absence of this sector, it's possible that you or your family will have difficulties in attracting recognition which is what often leads to success. This is especially the case if you or your family are involved in businesses or ventures that are dependent upon recognition and marketing.

Whether you are looking for that next promotion, become recognised as the expert in your field or want to outshine your competition in any job or business that comes to you, the energy from the South can give you that competitive edge.

This fire energy that represents the height and heat of summer and the ability to be recognised for your hard work and dedication is just like the red phoenix, it symbolises the energy of great strength, resilience and transformation, as it is able to raise from its own ashes to reach greater heights.

An important consideration to the South is ensuring this area of your home is kept well lit. This helps to keep the fire energy associated with the South charged and invigorated, supporting you with promotion, and being recognised for your efforts with material rewards into your life.

When enhancing your Fame & Reputation area of your home, this area also works hand-in-hand with the Career / Business / Life Path section of your space (front centre part of the space nearest the front door), which is directly opposite the Fame & Reputation side of your space. Be sure to enhance both of these sides simultaneously to get the results you desire, especially with respect to your Fame & Reputation in your business.

Enhancements could include candles and a tall lamp, these are, in particular, considered ideal for this purpose.

Your space should largely focus on your inner light, so find art that really speaks to your heart.

SOUTH WEST- LOVE, MARRIAGE & RELATIONSHIPS

Element: Earth
Magic Number: 2
Season: Summer into Autumn
Colour: Pink / Red / Yellow

Associated with marriage, partnership, friends, colleagues and how we relate to people in general. The most yin trigram, it represents flexibility, yielding and commitment. When both partners are flexible and take the other into consideration, a strong partnership emerges. This corner also refers to the relationship we have with ourselves.

Good for being caring, patient and compassionate; increases the desire to be practical and down-to-earth. It is the ideal chi for improving the quality of whatever you do.

Love, marriage, romance, personal and professional relationships are associated with the South West sector. The earth element is helpful for deepening all kinds of relationships.

Focus on creating an energy in your surroundings that will be a positive influence on you to achieve what you are looking for. Adding items in pairs in these areas are important if you want to spend your life with someone special.

Other enhancements could include porcelain bowls or pictures of mountains, for example. If you are single, a pair of ducks or pictures of love birds will support you in attracting love here.

WEST- LOVE, MARRIAGE & RELATIONSHIPS

Element: Metal
Magic Number: 7
Season: Autumn
Colour: White / Silver / Grey / Copper

Good for feeling joyful, celebrating and associated with being playful, seeking fun and enjoying the pleasures of life.

The West Sector represents joy, fullness, imagination and legacy creation. The luck of this area relates to creativity as well as children of the household and fertility.

If there is anything you are trying to get off the ground, such as a new business venture, particular attention to the West area of your office will support you in your venture.

Being associated with the stimulation of creative energies, the West is also a powerful area for artists and writers.

Utilising rainbow colours, lights and pictures as well as earth elements, earth objects and integrating colours of yellow, beige, silver, white or grey will also be supportive for activating this corner to stimulate creative flow.

In order to activate and enhance the West corner to improve and protect your family's happiness and good fortune, develop new artistic projects, or pursue having children or adding to your family, use metal elements, such as computers, wind chimes or bells. This corner also benefits by the addition of metal elements and metal colours, such as white and grey as well as earth colours of tan, beige, terracotta and ochre or yellow.

Other earth elements such as crystals and vases can also protect the children and guard them against injury, promoting the family's well-being. Crystals, images of mountains, globes and maps are also all excellent activators for the west sector, and in particular for anyone who makes a living by speaking such as actors, news reporters, speakers, podcasters, and politicians. This is also a wonderful area to display your children's art, paint, sculpt or work on any artistic endeavours.

NORTH WEST – HELPFUL PEOPLE & TRAVEL

Element: Metal

Magic Number: 6
Season: Autumn into Winter
Colour: Grey / Black / White

The North West sector is one of the critical areas of Feng Shui. When this is positively activated, you will have people who help you and who make introductions for you. One of the most supportive of all, especially when you need someone to help you.

Specifically, this corner will bring you luck through supportive mentors which will enable you to get ahead, be introduced to the right people, or be supported through their influence, guidance and assistance. This is also the sector that represents support, guidance, and love from close friends and unseen helpers, and denotes letting go of everything and everyone that doesn't serve you.

A good direction for being in charge, dignified and responsible; increases the desire to organise, plan ahead, be respected and have integrity. Helpful for greater wisdom and clearer intuition; it represents experience and maturity, finding it easy to win people's trust.

NORTH – SELF, CAREER, WORK & LIFE'S JOURNEY

Element: Water
Magic Number: 6
Season: Winter
Colour: Black / Deep Dark Blue

The North sector is the corner that relates to prosperity, opportunity, career, income and the flow of life. Whilst many Feng Shui enthusiasts like to focus on the wealth corner (South East) to make money, the South East is far more lucrative if the money earned is through the investments of stocks or increased savings amassing to financial assets.

The North, however, is much more related to the money you earn, business opportunities that arise and career advancement. To put this into perspective, look at the South East as relating to accrued money compared to your week in, week out earnings, income, and your business or career success that corresponds to the North corner.

Whilst financial stability and income create the foundations for you to build a life for yourself, the North isn't just about money. There are some other important elements of the North which make it even more powerful to support you. This direction also increases the desire to be flexible, find peace, study, develop yourself, improve health and be different.

You can activate the North sector of your home or living room with a fountain or a picture of water. Whether you like aquariums, fountains, or ponds, using these can help boost your reputation at work, improve your business, increase your income or bring newly found sources of income to you.

NORTH EAST – SELF, CAREER, WORK & LIFE'S JOURNEY

Element: Earth
Magic Number: 8
Season: Winter into Spring
Colour: Blue / Green / Brown

The North East is the corner of wisdom, knowledge, education, decision making, studying and writing. It represents a mountain of personal strength, resourcefulness, self-mastery, and self-control. It's also the link between a calm and intelligent mind.

To support the household with this corner, adding additional lighting will help energise the earth's energy. Other earth objects, including stones, crystals or globes of the earth can also support you in feeling inspired and achieving a sense of satisfaction. When it comes to the use of colour; yellow, beige and taupe colours are super effective for supporting you in 'grounding' your mind and gaining the clarity you need for effective decision making.

Good for being motivated, driven and outgoing; increases the desire to seize the moment, win, compete, learn, be decisive, clear-minded and adventurous. This chi is sharp, quick to change, making it good to make a deal and trading. It is also good for clearing your mind, helping you be more decisive and able to think about a new direction in life.

EAST – FAMILY & NEW BEGINNINGS

Element: Wood
Magic Number: 3
Season: Spring
Colour: Green / Blue

The East corner is full of life and great vitality as it promotes strong health, growth and vigorous energy. It's symbolic of our loving family relationships, honesty, forgiveness and the foundations of life, all of which can impact every member of the household. It is symbolised by the element of wood, the colour brown and the number three, as well as being known as the place of the dragon.

You can use the East corner to improve growth in your life, boosting your health and for seeing your family grow and prosper. However, if you are currently experiencing any health complaints, or perhaps you don't feel as healthy as you know you could feel, look for problems in the East corner of the house, living room, or your bedroom as this may provide valuable insights for you.

With the East being a wood element, adding water and fountains will help stimulate your life with new opportunities as well as strengthen the progress in your life. Therefore, just like plants need water, the East corner is perfect for some form of fountain to feed the flow of opportunities in your life, increased health and vitality. It will also become a positive enhancement in family relationships.

Like plants in general, trees are a wonderful source to bring in vitality, growth and support to your home. Adding big wood to your home in the form of a newly planted tree is a great way to add momentum and personal growth, as long as they are maintained and kept alive.

SOUTH EAST SECTOR: WEALTH & PROSPERITY

Element: Wood
Magic Number: 4

Season: Spring into Summer
Colour: Purple / Gold / Green / Blue / Red

The South East is the corner most often associated with wealth in Feng Shui. The primary wealth sector in any home is one of the most sought-after sectors to master concerning what most people, retrospectively believe, makes the world go around; wealth and prosperity.

This area is most associated with accumulated wealth rather than earning ability through a job, for example. Accumulated wealth means savings, investments or retirement funds, not a salary. If you have a bedroom, dining room, front door, bedroom or office in the South East, count yourself extremely lucky as this is a great location for you. Be sure to activate it.

When enhancing the wealth and prosperity section of your home or office, give attention to cultivating a strong feeling of gratitude for all the fortune in your life as this gratitude lends itself to allowing more wealth to flow to you.

You can enhance the area with either water (which feeds wood) or wooden elements such as a water fountain, a money tree plant or a bamboo plant. You can also use objects that remind you of money, including pictures of money, a picture of a check for any amount you can imagine, or items that make you feel wealthy, to reinforce that corner of your home.

Every room in your house has its own money corner. You may want to reinforce the positive chi in the money corner of your home office, your living room, or other places you spend a lot of time. You may also add a fountain to the wealth corner of your yard for increased fortune.

CENTRE: UNITY

Element: Wood
Magic Number: 5
Season: Spring into Summer
Colour: Yellow / Brown / Orange

This Centre is the heart and soul of your home; what happens in this area affects all members of the family. It is considered a neutral area or unity, a perfect balance of Yin and Yang energy.

Each of the surrounding sections all have their own individual role to play as this vital nourishing and supportive energy circulates and gathers in the Centre.

A well-balanced Centre is the epitome of good Feng Shui, producing a constant, gentle, auspicious supply of wonderful energy to all and when all aspects of life are in their right proportions, we will feel at peace.

The Centre represents this ideal. Hence, when we create balance and flow in the Centre of our space, we feel in harmony and fully experience the benefits of our efforts which enhance every area of our life.

You should focus your efforts in the centre of your space when you're feeling ungrounded or generally unsettled. The energy radiated from the centre of your home should be nourishing and protective.

The best use for this area of your home is a dining room or family living room.

I AM
FOCUSED AND
TAKING
INSPIRED ACTION
EVERY DAY

THE 4D VISION BOARD

SET YOUR HOME UP AS A POWERFUL 4D VISION BOARD

Have you done a vision board before? If you are familiar with manifestation and law of attraction ideas, creating a vision board that captures all your wishes won't be a new concept to you.

Usually, it involves pasting exciting magazine clippings of your long-for holiday destination, what your dream house looks like, a fancy car you'd love, a passionate partner, a big pile of cash, and of course affirmations and keywords of your future desires. Then, you'd put this vision board somewhere visible that keeps reminding you of your lust-worthy goals and vision for the year.

Sometimes, it's effective. Sometimes, it's not. Want to know why? The answer is simple, these desires are not intentional enough. Those images on your vision board are great, but they are not aligned with your powerful personal energy number and the strongest direction of energy flow for you to fully tap in to.

If you want your vision board to transform into a magnet to attract everything you desire and more, you need to align it with the energy of fortune by using the tips and tools that Creative Feng Shui is based upon. Going forward, you will learn how to place your powerful intentions and goals in the right energy space, in the right direction, at the right time.

Our home is our most precious and intimate space, so designing our space with intention whilst aligning it with positive energy, is what Creative Feng Shui will help you to do. The aim here is to turn your home into a four-dimensional vision board and to do that, involves utilising everything you have been provided with so far in this book.

Creating a 4D vision board involves specifically knowing the best places to attract your vision (i.e. aligning the wealth energy direction when setting wealth-related goals). When you do this, you will automatically infuse the highest positive energy into your space, and you can enhance your intentions furthermore.

There are nine life fields associated with the 4D vision board, and the ultimate aim is to collate the everything you have learnt so far about the magic map, the life wheel and your personal energy number to produce a real-life version of what this looks like for you.

To spark your imagination, let me give you some ideas. Perhaps you're looking to boost your career? Sell your home? Find a new relationship? Or maybe add more travel into your life? At this point, you want to be finding out where your intention falls within your home layout and from there, start adding the elements that will contribute to driving that intention forward. For example, if you want to add more travel into your life, you can focus on this area on your vision board. Enhance your vision by adding images of the very places you would like to go, maps of the areas you may want to travel in and any helpful people that will support you in bringing this goal into fruition.

When you look at your vision board it should be seen as your physical map and your tour guide which specifically tells you where you are going, what you want to attract, and how you are going to do it.

Ultimately, you will have a living, breathing, in-depth and very specific vision board which is consistently evolving with you, your business and your home. It's time to up-level your vision board techniques so that you can call in everything you desire and more straight away. Here's what to do:

SET YOUR INTENTIONS

How do you know where you're going, if you don't know where you're going?

An intention is the starting point of every dream. It is the creative power that fulfils all of our needs; whether for money, success, relationships, health or wellbeing. An intention is a directed impulse of consciousness that contains the seed of thought, aspiration or outcome you desire and that you would like to see emerge. Like real seeds, intentions can't grow if you hold on to them.

When you become intentional and focus your efforts towards these intentions, they can support, develop and grow into your consciousness so that they can thrive - just like you.

So, it's important to set your intentions for every area of your life before you even create your vision board. The fundamental part of this powerful process is to be extremely intentional and focused about what you want for every area of your life, personally and professionally. Therefore, start by setting 4 intentions (2 intentions for your personal life and 2 intentions for your business/career) for the following areas:

- Success & Money
- Personal & Professional Relationships
- Health & Wellbeing
- Self-Development & Personal Growth

Example:

My intention is to invite an abundance of wealth, happiness and contentment into my life and business.

CREATE YOUR VISION BOARD

I highly recommend hand-crafting your vision board in a way that feels achievable for you. The more love, thought, feelings and emotions put into creating this, the more you'll bring your vision to life.

Some clients have painted their vision board, others have used good old-fashioned coloured paper and a Pritt Stick! My tip here is to use something which you can easily adjust, replace and remove as you'll be updating this on a regular basis.

Create the vision board with plenty of space to add your goals, images, quotes and activations. Go BIG! My board is A1 in size, and I used coloured paper to create the appropriate life sections.

Aim for something like this:

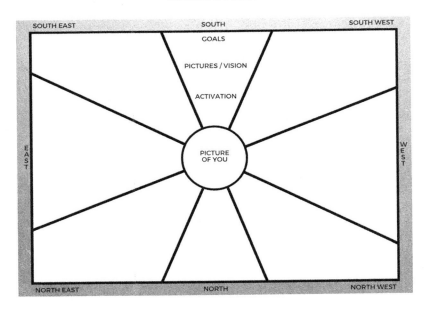

Top Tips:

Make sure that you add the compass directions and add South to the top like the example above. Also, ensure that you have a gold frame and a white line separating each section and the centre (use the black lines above as your guide).

You can access a template and tutorial on creating your vision board at: www.sarahstone.com/book-resources.

ADD YOUR GOALS AND DESIRES

Find your 4 best directions for Success & Money, Personal & Professional Relationships, Health & Wellbeing and

Personal Growth based upon your Personal Energy Number we calculated earlier in the book:

PERSONAL ENERGY NUMBER	SUCCESS & MONEY FLOW	HEALTH & VITALITY	PERSONAL & PROFESSIONAL RELATIONSHIPS	PERSONAL GROWTH
1	SOUTH EAST	EAST	SOUTH	NORTH
2	NORTH EAST	WEST	NORTH WEST	SOUTH WEST
3	SOUTH	NORTH	SOUTH EAST	EAST
4	NORTH	SOUTH	EAST	SOUTH EAST
5 (FEMALE)	SOUTH WEST	NORTH WEST	WEST	NORTH EAST
5 (MALE)	NORTH EAST	WEST	NORTH WEST	SOUTH WEST
6	WEST	NORTH EAST	SOUTH WEST	NORTH WEST
7	NORTH WEST	SOUTH WEST	NORTH EAST	WEST
8	NORTH EAST	NORTH WEST	WEST	NORTH EAST
9	EAST	SOUTH EAST	NORTH	SOUTH

Create very specific (but not limited) goals that are aligned with your personal energy number direction and the overall Bagua map for the best possible results. For example; if your personal success area is in the South East, your goals should include goals for 'Wealth & Abundance' as this is an extremely strong area for you.

I recommend that you start with your Success Direction first. Place your goals on the top outer edge of the board, then place images that represent your goal, who you are inspired by or someone who is already achieving what you would like to achieve. Then all you have to do is activate your board with a nature element, symbol, shape, object or quantum colour which works for the direction you are focusing on.

Once you feel happy with how your vision board feels, you can do the same with the remaining 3 fortune areas.

CREATE A 4D VISION IN YOUR HOME

When your board has your goals, images and activations, you're now ready to activate your office, living space and bedroom with powerful intentions to enhance everything you've started to call into your life.

To achieve the best outcome with this, write your goals on beautiful index cards (activation cards) or use lovely stationery and place them in your more fortunate areas of your home. Your personal goals should be placed in your living area and bedroom, and your business goals should be placed in your office.

When you feel that you don't want to put these goals in view, place them in a beautiful envelope and indicate on the front that they are for the universe.

To enhance your personal activation cards, you can:

- Add an image that represents your aspirations

- Add an image of someone who has achieved what you would like to achieve
- Add symbols and activations that represent your goal
- Place them in the relevant direction of your more fortunate energy

Within your office, living room and bedroom, you can start to position your desk, chairs and even bed to face your best directions as it can now be applied to everything you do.

POSITION FOR SUCCESS

Once you have created your 4D Vision Board, ensure you position it in your success direction, somewhere where you can see it, check it and update it often.

SHOW GRATITUDE

When you achieve your goals, show your gratitude by writing 'THANK YOU', the date and sign your name. Then leave your gratitude on the board for 9 days before removing your goal and associated images so that you can create space for a new goal to call in.

I AM
FREE TO CHOOSE
TO LIVE AS I WISH
& GIVE PRIORITY
TO MY DESIRES

RESISTANCE & CHANGE

BE OPEN TO RESISTANCE & CHANGE

R esistance to change is normal. And it's ok to feel uneasy when things are changing fast, even when they're changing for the better!

It's the reason why I wanted to add in this section about resistance to change as it's likely to arise as you start to make some powerful changes in the flow of energy. This can show up because you're disrupting stagnant, blocked negative energy, therefore it may throw up feelings and emotions of frustration – making you question if this technique really works or is worth the feeling of 'disruption'. If you're feeling this at any stage of the process, stick with it, if you can feel a shift; you're already making the changes required to create a better flow of energy, and I can pretty much guarantee that it will be worth it in the long-run. *Lean in.*

Here are some other reasons why people feel some resistance when introducing Creative Feng Shui:

People who have a natural resistance to Feng Shui are often at odds with the natural rhythm of life, which is constantly in a state of change. To offer some reassurance here, change is completely natural and by making these adjustments, it can help you embrace more change as part of the cycle of life.

People see only what they want to see. We have selective vision and tend to ignore what doesn't please us. Our dreams and desires sometimes blind us to what we already have accomplished. For example, even if business improves in a slow but steady pace, we complain because we didn't land the multi-million-pound turnover yet.

There's sometimes a tendency to focus on failures when, in fact, there has been great progress and success. My aim is to encourage you to become more aware and open to celebrating your achievements at every stage of your progress.

Another reason is that people may not be ready to accept or want change. Sometimes we think that we want 'something,' but in truth, we either don't want to make any changes, or we aren't ready to accept change. The thing is, if you are supposed to do something, the universe will clear the way for it to happen (and quickly); but if you're not supposed to do something, it will place obstacles in your path to encourage you to find another route to achieve your goal.

Believe in divine timing. It's a hard one when you were expecting things to go one specific way in your mind… but divine timing is real. Everything happens in its own time.

Creative Feng Shui works best when you focus on improving a specific aspect of your life with intention. This could be finding a new romantic partner, scaling your business, or creating more family flow. Targeting a specific goal allows you to focus on the areas of your home or office where Shui Feng Shui improvements will be most effective. It's also helpful to remain flexible about the results of Creative Feng Shui changes since there might be an even better possibility that you haven't imagined.

My top tip if you're feeling resistance frequently, try some stretching, yoga or qigong every day because a flexible body lends itself to a more flexible mind.

9 POWERFUL ACTIVATIONS & ENHANCEMENTS

COLOUR

In Creative Feng Shui, each colour is considered to be an expression of one of the five feng shui elements: Fire, Earth, Metal, Water, and Wood. Each of these five elements contributes to a specific area of your home. The use of colour can bring fresh energy and help active a positive flow of energy.

SOUND

Sound, specifically music, is a powerful way to uplift the chi in any environment and to soothe stress in the home or office. Other sound makers such as wind chimes and tuning forks attract, or 'call-in' the positive energy flow into your home or workplace.

LIGHTING

Candles are a simple and beautiful way to bring more positive energy into your environment. They are best placed in the South, South West, North East and the Centre. This will keep the flow of energy in your home harmonious and healthy.

ART

Art of any kind, whether it is a painting, sculpture, or textiles, can enhance and activate positive energy. The selection of art should reflect positive images and feelings. The placement of your art depends on the area of the 'Magic Map' you want to enhance.

LIVING THINGS

Plants, fresh flowers, and animals add active chi. Pets bring wonderful energy, just be sure to keep items such as fish tanks, pet cages and sleeping areas clean.

WATER

To keep your life moving in its desired direction, place a water feature near your front door, inside or out. Features such as water fountains, fish tanks, and waterfalls stimulate the flow of energy in and around your home or workplace.

It is important to choose a sound of moving water that is soothing and tranquil rather than distracting and disruptive.

WIND-SENSITIVE OBJECTS

Enhancements such as wind chimes, weather vanes, and flags attract positive energy towards your home. They can also be used to help cure the missing areas of the 'Magic Map'.

MIRRORS

Mirrors can be used inside to reflect a pleasant view into a home or to symbolically move a wall and correct its shape; outside, they can be used to deflect a negative structure or unpleasant object.

CRYSTALS

Crystals represent energy from deep within the earth and can help you feel grounded. Hanging a clear faceted crystal in a window will attract the sparkle of the sun and its full spectrum of colour into your space - creating rainbows for your soul.

I AM
GRATEFUL
FOR EVERY
MOMENT
OF MY
LIFE

YOUR SEASONAL GUIDE

AUTUMN

Autumn is the best time to harvest and gather your ideas. Use this time to prepare yourself and your home for your future goals. Here are some Creative Feng Shui activities to help you take inspired action in Autumn:

Be mindful of anything you're storing up high. Clutter kept in these high places interferes with your 'high hopes.'

Your front door is where all your fortune and opportunities enter our lives, so use the back door to take out your rubbish. Also, don't store bins in any of your lucky directions as you're essentially putting your luck in the bin.

Avoid sitting anyone at one of the four corners of your table's four corners. It will make your guest feel 'on edge' during their meal.

Once a week, dedicate 10-15 minutes to removing photos, online files and emails you don't need. Some days you'll clear hundreds, other days you'll only do a few. The amount doesn't matter, just getting into a routine of clearing out what's no longer required to create space is the main focus.

Collect ideas for redecorating, planning a wedding or your future travel plans.

If your attention is being drawn to a particular room or project, know that this space likely corresponds with something in your life that you *really* want to change.

If you lack in confidence, grab your favourite crystal. Hold it while you concentrate on an intention to overcome your self-doubt, and then place it near you during the day. Your trusty crystal will reform your fear into courage and certainty. You've got this!

When you're 'calling in' something you really want, a new client, a new job, a new connection – your bedroom can help! Bedrooms are synonymous with all relationships, so consider artwork or imagery that reflects a meaningful relationship to you, and it will stimulate the energy around this for you.

If you are storing never-been-used things, find a way to use them now. And if you can't, explore the fear and worry behind why you have them. When you hoard stuff for years, it activates the idea that life won't get better. Donate what you don't want, let it go and trust the whatever you need will make its way to you. Create space for it to arrive.

Clean your windows. In Feng Shui windows represent the 'eyes' of the adults in the home. By washing windows, this clears your vision and 'opens our eyes' to greater possibilities.

WINTER

Winter is a time of stillness. Here are some Creative Feng Shui activities to help you take inspired action in Winter:

Utilise this time to nurture and pursue solo activities like starting meditation practice, journaling or a new hobby.

Make your bedroom cosy and romantic. Most people like to feel nestled into their bedrooms, completely secure and sheltered from the world. If your bedroom is large, create two or more cosy places to enjoy.

Match your art with the function of each room. Choose soothing, romantic art for your bedroom; lively, colourful art for the living room; and powerful, motivational art for your office.

Candles enhance energy by bringing light, stimulate your senses with scent, add warmth and colour into your home. They evoke feelings, emotions and allow you to create the perfect ambience for the mood you want to create.

Consider making your home a 'shoeless' house. Design a place to store shoes as this helps keep your home clean, yet symbolises leaving your worldly cares and concerns at the door.

Keep your front entrance in good repair. Paint, wash or spruce it up as soon as it shows signs of wear and tear.

Group a few plants together to activate networking opportunities.

How much of your stuff sits or lives on the ground? If you want to be on the rise, enhance this energy by placing something eye-catching above your eye level to suggest that you're scaling to new heights.

The universe gives you more of that you offer, so use the festivity of any season to hand out gold covered chocolate coins!

SPRING

Spring is a time for renewal and new beginnings. Here are some Creative Feng Shui activities to help you take inspired action in Spring:

It's a great time to start a detox, clear out your clutter, or begin a new routine. Think fresh action and new starts.

Keep your plant's leaves glossy and clean. It will help everyone 'breathe easy' as glossy leaves also give off Water energy, and Water energy will put you back in flow.

Lean into your intuition. Visit every room of your house and ask yourself:

Does this space contain a representation of where I want to be in 2-5 years?

What could be possibly holding me back?

Is there anything here blocking my success?

Looking for LOVE? Dedicate space for a partner now. Clear out a drawer or two for his/her stuff. Buy a new toothbrush and tend to the details of your lover's arrival, and the universe will get the hint!

Water equals money.

Water leak equals money leak.

Slow water leak equals slow, but steady, money leak.

Bottom line: Fix water leaks immediately!

Clutter under your bed breeds anxiety. An empty space here is advisable. However, if you need it for storage, let your soft stuff like bedding live here.

Spritz essential oils like ylang ylang or vetiver. Ylang ylang heals the heart, calms your inner child and soothes relationship issues. Vetiver centres and relaxes.

Creative Feng Shui works best when you make 1-2 changes at a time. This modern approach provides two advantages. One, you notice what works, what doesn't and how it makes you feel. Two, every improvement you make in your environment improves your energy which enhances your confidence to do more! The secret recipe to your momentum and success.

If you have any broken mirrors, remove them. Mirrors represent being able to see clearly, and a cracked mirror will fragment your perception of circumstances and situations.

SUMMER

Summer is a time for expansion, playfulness and completion. Here are some Creative Feng Shui activities to help you take inspired action in Summer:

Make time for outdoor activities and tap into ways that bring joy into your life.

Ever wished you were an influencer? Here's the good news – YOU ARE! Your personal chi is powerful and magnetic in your space. Shine your light and share an important message with the world. You are seen and heard.

If you are single and looking for LOVE, buy a bundle of peonies for your living room. When choosing colours, go for the softer shades of pink.

Find 9 things that have been in the same spot for 6 months or more and move them around. The simple act of rearranging gets energy back in sync with high vibrational living.

Fire is the element of excitement, passion and enthusiasm. It favours meeting people and making new connections. Let conversations linger, sit fireside and watch the flames dance.

Start a money jar and add to it daily. Wealth starts with your own consciousness of abundance, and seeing money grow on a daily basis will attract more money to you.

When sunshine and Swarovski crystals meet, rainbow rays dance around the room. Create rainbows in the South area of your home.

If you can see a bathroom from your bed, shut its door – especially before falling asleep at night. Otherwise, the toilet, sink and drains will take your mood and energy 'down the drain' too.

What hangs on your walls, hangs in your mind. So your vision board is a 'yay'. Once you've reached your goals, be sure to change it up so that your board lives and breathes with you - helping you create and live what you love.

I AM
CELEBRATING
AN ABUNDANCE
OF WEALTH

THE POWER OF COLOUR

Colours signify an important component to the way in which we can activate our vision board, our environment and the energy associated with Creative Feng Shui.

As you will have discovered by now, each direction is associated with supportive quantum colours that enhance our ability to increase the flow to that specific direction. This awareness is something which Creatives and Interior Designers find to be of great value when it comes to decorating rooms and impacting the homes they design positively for the occupants.

In alignment with traditional Feng Shui, the meaning of colour goes a lot deeper when it comes to creating a desired outcome; whether that be good health, increased success or protecting your income and wealth.

The power of colour and how it supports you is related to your personal energy number, your power directions and nature elements attached to when you were born. Understanding and using these colours correctly will create harmony, and balance energy in your life, bringing health, wealth and happiness.

The use of colour is the quickest way to start changing your energy using Creative Feng Shui, so here's a deeper insight into what certain colours mean for you:

VIOLET / PURPLE

Associated with wealth and prosperity in Creative Feng Shui. These colours inspire and invite abundance and fortune. It is also deeply connected with spiritual awareness and is the colour for physical and mental healing.

Purple tones make for ideal colours to be used in a meditation to help you connect to your divine wisdom.

YELLOW

Associated with the centre of health in Creative Feng Shui. **Yellow** represents warmth, friendliness and happiness. It also helps you to stand within your personal power.

Like the sun giving us warmth and life, yellow does the same for our environment. This uplifting and cheerful colour is best suited for the family room or the children's room.

ORANGE

Associated with the centre of health in Creative Feng Shui. **Orange** is believed to strengthen concentration and sharpen your creative skills. It is used to give a sense of purpose and organisation. Ideal for your study or office or if you want to invite a little spontaneity into your life or need to break through a creative block.

WHITE

Associated with helpful people and travel in Creative Feng Shui. **White** is the colour of purity. It represents confidence, poise and trustworthiness. There are many shades of white, and in Feng Shui, they symbolise purity and precision. White is related to the metal element and inspires clarity and cleansing.

Helps you align with your highest good, in mind, body, soul and spirit.

GREY

Associated with creativity, children and joy in Creative Feng Shui. Grey is a mixture of white and black, like Yin and Yang. White is clarity, while black is wisdom. Grey is related to the Helpful People and Travel area of the Bagua map. If you need some support or want to travel more, this is a great colour to use.

BLUE

Associated with water energy, support inner work, helping us to concentrate, contemplate, meditate and handle creative endeavours. Blue is connected to the self-knowledge and skilfulness in Feng Shui. This colour helps you with self-cultivation and gaining understanding.

Creating a relaxing atmosphere, the colour has a soothing effect that helps your mind to quieten down and your body to heal. It's the colour of peace and trust.

Navy blue relates to wisdom, and all blues represent adventure and exploration.

RED

Associated with fame and reputation in Creative Feng Shui. **Red** embodies truth and virtue. It is a positive and passionate colour representing vibrancy, joy and happiness. The most auspicious colour in Feng Shui, the power of red is obvious.

Red can be used to invite prosperity, good health, and luck. Red is related to fire, energy, and passion. A little goes a long way, so don't be afraid to add a little red into your home to inspire and revitalise you.

PINK

Associated with love, marriage and relationships in Creative Feng Shui. Pink is a softer colour that can invite feminine energy. Pink can invite partnerships, love and help cultivate self-care into your life. Pink is a wonderful colour to add to your home if you're looking for a romantic relationship or if you want to work on your relationship with yourself.

BLACK

Associated with career and life path in Creative Feng Shui. Full of sophistication and mystery, wisdom is evoked with the colour black. If you mix all the colours of the rainbow together, you get black. Hence, black is inclusive and contains knowledge of all things. The colour black is also related to the element of water. Water is vast and deep. It flows, connects and provides life. Use black sparingly and wisely to open your home up to more wisdom.

It adds depth and strength to your living space and holds the energy of protection and power.

GREEN

Associated with family and new beginnings in Creative Feng Shui. **Green** is associated with wood energy, the energy of growth, decisiveness and action. It can motivate internal change, and it's the colour of hope, rebirth, growth, and health so make the best out of the energies of this nourishing colour and use several of its tones.

This calming Feng Shui colour brings healing vibrations and balance to your body.

YOUR EMERGENCY TOOLKIT

CALL IN LOVE

The colour pink represents love in Feng Shui. If pink isn't your thing, you can complement it with shades of nudes for a more sophisticated look.

If you are a female, looking for a loving, romantic partner, place 2 rose quartz hearts in the South West area of your home. It's important to create the energy of partnership around you. Otherwise, you are continually enforcing singularity.

Add a second chair to a sitting area, double up on night-stands and surround yourself with pairs of everything. Use aromatherapy sprays or candles to make sure the space always smells lovely, and peonies are also the perfect flower activation to help you attract your perfect partner.

IMPROVE EXISTING RELATIONSHIPS

To decrease stress and arguing in your home, check your surroundings. Ensure that you have no sharp objects on show. Display smiling photos of yourself as a couple and your family in the hallways, kitchen or other high-traffic areas.

To improve existing relationships, strengthen the South West areas of your home, along with the Fire element in the South. Bring in images and symbols that you associate with love and meaningful relationships. Decorate in pairs, such as two complementary candlesticks or lamps.

In your bedroom, ensure that there is equal presence. For example, ensure that you both have a bedside table and lamp for balance in your relationship.

In order to enhance the general relationships between everyone in your home or in the home of your extended family, you want to start by activating the East area in your living room and family room.

Consider incorporating elements of Wood, such as flowers, plants and any wooden objects or flower artwork to powerfully enhance the energy here.

IMPROVE RELATIONSHIPS WITH YOUR CHILDREN

The area to focus on here is the West area of your house, garden and all major rooms. We will cover this association in more detail in a later part of this book, but for now, you can already start to activate your West areas by placing images of children, children playing or personal pictures of you with your own children and grandchildren.

To create positivity in a child's bedroom, display happy images of their secret friends and allies on the wall or beside their bed. Cartoon movie images work very well for this, or having the child draw the characters themselves is also a really beneficial activity for them to do.

Consider creating the feeling of tenderness in their bedrooms with images of fairies and dragonflies. You can also place images painted by your children and add a laughing Buddha as it's good for this direction.

When it comes to the relationships with your children, be careful not to use too many dark and aggressive messages in their bedrooms, like 'do not enter' or 'keep out' signs for example. Negative messages will influence your relationship, so ensure that you try to positively influence the harmony not just in their room, but in the entire house.

CALL IN MONEY

Want to attract money? To increase your bank account, repair any water leaks and remove all stagnant water from your property. Whatever the state of your water, your finances mirror those.

To bring in more wealth and abundance, it's important to create a vibrant, healthy, inspiring and clutter-free home. Bubbling fountains are important wealth adjustments in Feng Shui because they stimulate prosperity, fortune and symbolise money flowing to you.

It's best not to display water-based artwork or mirrors higher than your nose, which carries the same significance in Feng Shui. For most of us, that means no mirrors or water scenes above the bed.

ACTIVATE SUCCESS

In your home, place specific pictures and images that represent your financial and success goals in this area. Put your 4D Vision Board in your Success Direction in your bedroom, living room, and/or office (where you spend 5 hours or more a day). Personal accomplishments and any professional degrees you have earned can go here. Pictures of people who are successful in the area of your intentions can be a valuable addition to your Success area.

In your office, place your profit goal and representations of new projects you are working on. Success magazines relating to your field would be excellent here.

Awards, certifications, degrees that represent your success can be great activates to invite an abundance of success.

CALL IN CREATIVE FLOW

Remove anything that no longer serves a purpose that is in your highest and best interest. In other words, clutter is stagnant energy that blocks the creative feng shui energy flow and instead drains energy from you.

The West of your office represents blooming projects, creativity and completion of anything you set your mind to. It is a great area to energise with white, metal and grey tones (for clarity) and use citrus scents to stimulate your senses.

The best way to activate this area is to keep it well-lit and with a continuous flow of fresh air. Activate the energy of creation and completion by applying Creative Feng Shui symbols like a 6-rod metal chime that will motivate the completion and success of your projects.

ENHANCE BETTER SLEEP

It is extremely beneficial when you sleep with the crown of your head against one of your four personal best directions. Not only will you sleep better, but you tap into the good energy coming to you all night.

UPGRADE YOUR TRAVEL DESIRES

Want to be treated like a VIP when travelling? Want more travel opportunities?

Activating your 'Helpful People & Travel' of your home is possible with the help of Creative Feng Shui. The best way to activate your travel luck is to use a crystal shell. Keep this lucky shell under your mattresses (more towards pillow side) to boost travel opportunities abroad.

If you would like more global clients, speaking or business opportunities around the world, place a globe in the North West area of your 4D Vision Board to call this in.

How to Use the Glossary

Each term in the glossary includes a detailed definition. Many terms have additional variations of spelling, terminology and references. The 'also called' directs you to another term in the glossary explaining to the definition and connection a little more. 'See' refers to multiple words in the definition for further reference in the glossary.

Activation

To activate something is to start it off, trigger it, or set it in motion.

Auspicious

A term frequently used in Feng Shui, Astrology, and divination to denote favourable, desirable and beneficial influences and successful results.

Bagua Map

The Feng Shui Bagua is one of the main tools used in Feng Shui used to analyse the energy of any given space, be it home, office, or garden. Bagua is the Feng Shui energy map of your space that shows you which areas of your home or office are connected to specific areas of your life.

Book of Changes (I Ching)

I Ching (pronounced ee ching) is an interpretation manual known as the Book of Changes which were first used as an oral tradition long before it was ever written down in a text format. Today, the I Ching has been translated hundreds if not thousands of times, and it has multiple uses in feng shui and other practices. The I Ching is an art form of divination that is over 5,000 years old and still widely practiced in China.

Chi

Sometimes described as the cosmic breath, or as the vital principle. It is the essence of the principles of heaven and earth, of time and space, it is the force of change and transformation.

Clutter

Clutter is low, stagnant, and confusing energy that constantly drains energy from you. Depending on the feng shui area of your home where your clutter is located, it can also negatively influence, or even completely block, the flow of energy and events in many areas of your life.

Compass

A *compass* is an instrument used for navigation and orientation that shows direction relative to the cardinal geographic directions (or points). The Feng Shui compass is used by a Feng Shui practitioner to determine the precise direction of a structure or power direction.

Constructive Cycle

Refers to the cycle in which each of the five elements creates, nourishes, and enhances the subsequent one as we observe the elements in a clockwise circular pattern. They do so in the following sequence:

Wood enhances Fire.

Fire enhances Earth.

Earth enhances Metal.

Metal enhances Water.

Water enhances Wood.

Controlling Cycle

Refers to the cycle in which each of the five elements controls, weakens or dominates another in a pentagram pattern as they are viewed in their natural circular diagram. They do this in the following sequence:

Wood breaks up Earth.

Earth absorbs Water.

Water puts out Fire.

Fire melts Metal.

Metal cuts Wood.

Destructive Cycle

Refers to the cycle in which each of the five elements controls, weakens or dominates another in a pentagram pattern as they are viewed in their natural circular diagram. They do this in the following sequence: Refers to the cycle in which each of the five elements controls, weakens or dominates another in a pentagram pattern as they are viewed in their natural circular diagram. They do this in the following sequence:

Wood breaks up Earth.

Earth absorbs Water.

Water puts out Fire.

Fire melts Metal.

Metal cuts Wood.

Earth

Yellow is the colour representing Earth, and the square shapes depict it. The season is late summer, and the emotion is sympathy.

East

One of the four cardinal directions, signifying new growth. The related element is Wood and is considered to be the starting point of the Five Elements energy cycle.

Elements

The five different kinds of emotional energy represented by wood, fire, earth, metal, and water. The most important aspect of the five elements is how they are related to each other as a constructive and de-constructive cycle.

Here is the best way to see how these work together:

Wood feeds fire, breaks up the earth and exhausts water.

Fire generates earth, melts metal and exhausts wood.

Earth creates metal, absorbs water and exhausts fire.

Metal holds water, cuts wood and exhausts earth.

Water feeds wood, puts fire out and exhausts metal.

Energy flow

Energy and energy flow is the key concept in Feng Shui. It is the movement of life force within our living space or body, which can affect our wellbeing either auspiciously or inauspiciously. Feng Shui concerns itself with the movement and containment of energy to create the most beneficial support for a person in their environment. The quality of energy is determined by its flow and the frequency of its vibration. By raising that frequency, we improve its quality and beneficial influence.

Enhancement

An object, talisman, ritual, prayer, action or intention used to achieve the greatest balance, harmony, and the most beneficial qi/chi in a space, or to suppress, neutralize or dissipate negative or stagnant energies or qi/chi.

Feng Shui

Feng shui is, first and foremost, energy work. It is used as a tool to open up powerful energy channels in your environment to help it attract stronger positive energy and create a more harmonious, powerful space. This, in turns, nourishes and strengthens your own energy.

Five Elements

The five different kinds of emotional energy represented by wood, fire, earth, metal, and water. The most important aspect of the five elements is how they are related to each other as a constructive and de-constructive cycle.

Here is the best way to see how these work together:

Wood feeds fire, breaks up the earth and exhausts water.

Fire generates earth, melts metal and exhausts wood.

Earth creates metal, absorbs water and exhausts fire.

Metal holds water, cuts wood and exhausts earth.

Water feeds wood, puts fire out and exhausts metal.

Inauspicious

A term frequently used in Feng Shui to denote unfavourable, undesirable, harmful influences and unsuccessful results.

Luck

Good or bad fortune, composed of heaven luck, earth luck, and human luck as it relates to Feng Shui.

Magic Square

The foundation of all Feng Shui numerology. An arrangement of the number 1-9 on a grid, so that in a straight line always add up to 15. Each number has an association with a fortunate direction and nature element. This grid is then laid over the layout of your space to see the flow of energy there.

Metal

One of the Five Elements represented by the colour white or grey. Its movement is still, inward and contracting. Metal energy is very precise, logical, and has leadership qualities. It represents the West sector of the Bagua with number 7 and Northwest with number 6, spherical shapes, Autumn season, and the emotion is grief.

Numerology

The symbolism of numbers in Creative Feng Shui is significant. Numerology is a study of numbers in your life. You can uncover information about the world and also each individual person by using Numerology. Numerology is seen as a universal language of numbers.

Pendulum

A pendulum is a weight suspended from a pivot so that it can swing freely. Used within Creative Feng Shui to help energy test a space.

Poison Arrow

Poison Arrow refers to all types of negative, harmful, and inauspicious energy both indoors and out. This can include a straight alignment of landform features such as trees, poles, or nearby buildings, sharp corners, sharp objects, stagnant water, beams and trusses, and gravesites.

Power Position

In Creative Feng Shui, the Power Position is the physical position in the room, which has the most fortunate flow of chi, based on your personal energy number.

Productive Cycle

Refers to the cycle in which each of the five elements creates, nourishes, enhances the subsequent one as we observe the elements in a clockwise circular pattern. They do so in the following sequence: Wood enhances Fire, Fire enhances Earth, Earth enhances Metal, Metal enhances Water, and Water enhances Wood. Also called: Creative Cycle, Constructive Cycle, Five Element Productive Cycle.

Qi Gong

Spiritual exercises to stimulate your chi and allow it to find its own natural flow within your energy field.

Red Phoenix

A symbolic animal of Form School and one of four Celestial Animals, the red phoenix represents water features in front of a structure in the Form School armchair metaphor. It also represents Summer and the colour red. Also called Phoenix, Red Bird. See Armchair, Celestial Animals, Form School, Four Emblems

Reductive Cycle

Refers to the cycle in which each of the five elements reduces the previous element as we view them in their natural circular, counter-clockwise pattern. They do this in the following sequence: Wood reduces Water, Water reduces Metal, Metal reduces Earth, Earth reduces Fire, Fire reduces Wood. Also called Five Element Reducing Cycle. See Earth, Five Elements, Metal, Water, Wood

Remedy

An object, talisman ritual, prayer, action or intention used to achieve the greatest balance, harmony, and the most beneficial qi/chi in a space, or to suppress, neutralize or dissipate negative or stagnant energies or qi/chi. See Adjustment, Chi, Cure, Enhancement, Remedy, Qi

Seasons

Forms part of and compliments the five elements and compass direction as you can see here:

ELEMENT	SEASON	SHAPE	COLOUR	DIRECTION
FIRE	SUMMER	TRIANGLE / PYRAMID	RED / PURPLE	SOUTH
EARTH	LATE SUMMER	SQUARE	YELLOW	SOUTH WEST CENTER NORTH EAST
METAL	AUTUMN	ROUND	WHITE	WEST NORTH WEST
WATER	WINTER	WAVY ASYMMETRIC	BLACK / NAVY BLUE	NORTH
WOOD	SPRING	TALL / RECTANGULAR	GREEN / LIGHT BLUE	EAST SOUTH EAST

Shui

Translates as water / fortune.

Space Clearing

Refers to any method used to disperse negative, stagnant, or inauspicious qi/chi or energy in a space, whether residual or current. Methods include, but are not limited to, the use of sound, incense, smudging, ritual, dance, pendulum techniques, or simply intention.

Vision Board

A vision board is a visualisation and manifestation tool which refers to a board of intention, goals, images and Feng Shui enhancements and activations. Calls in your deepest desires.

Water

Relates to going with the flow, being flexible and regenerating deeply. It is symbolised by the colour black and asymmetrical shapes. The associated season is winter, and the emotion is fear.

Wood

The colour green, and pillar and column shapes represent wood, and the representation can be found in wood furniture, plants and plant-based materials. The season is spring, and the emotion is anger.

Yin and Yang

Yin and yang are the opposite and complementary terms that can be used to describe anything. They are negative and positive phases in the cycle of energy. Generally, Yang refers to anything that makes you feel active, energetic, quick, alert, focused etc. Yin describes anything that helps you relax, slow down, open your mind, be creative and is more restful. What originates with yang is received and completed by yin. They are inseparable, and the one implies the other.

I AM
SURROUNDED
BY SUPPORTIVE
PEOPLE WHO
BELIEVE IN ME

WITH GRATITUDE

I am so grateful to everyone that has supported me in bringing this book to life. Special and heartfelt thanks have to start with Abigail Horne, without whom none of 'this' would have been remotely conceivable or achievable without her relentless support and guidance. Thank you for always seeing the limitless possibilities that I couldn't quite see for myself at times. Thank you for being my rock, sister-from-another-mister, business bestie and Hollywood tour guide. Your huge heart, unwavering kindness, loyalty and friendship never ceases to amaze me. With every inch of my heart, Thank You, I love you!

To the intuitive soul who healed and transformed my outlook on life, Nichola Sproson, without you manifesting an epic Feng Shui Expert back in 2019, I know for a fact that Creative Feng Shui would not be making its way out into the world. Thank you for teaching me how to heal, creating the space for me to safely realise my true purpose and guiding me on this transformational process with love, compassion and of course, the mighty tuning forks. You're definitely the yin and my yang. You are a real-life guardian forking angel, and I appreciate you more than words can say, thank you for always putting your faith in me, I cherish you.

To the missing piece of my puzzle, Kezia Luckett. Over the years we've both known there was a special connection in some way, now we know why. There's no doubt that without you being there and drilling into me that I was destined for bigger things, I'd still be hiding and probably stopped believing that I was made for more. You've instilled this within me deeper than ever, and through you, I've found the gift that I now get to share with the world. It's priceless and I will be forever indebted for your trust, belief, kindness, friendship and open heart you continue to share. Thank you my lovely. I feel completely honoured to have you in my life.

To the bundle of positivity Lucy Crane, what would I do without you and your endless support, help with words and getting this book DONE? Your enthusiasm, positive encouragement and friendship have guided me through the panic, confusion and tough days. A thousand thank yous for being there every step of the way; you mean the world to me. Thank you.

To my superstar birthday twin, Mrs D. You'll never really know how much of an impact you've truly had on my life. You've taught me the value of loyalty, true friendship, honesty, difficult conversations and taking action. Thank you for being my pillar of strength when I had nothing within me to keep going, I truly value our friendship, and I'm so proud to have you in my life. You'll be glad to know that the **BIG GIRL PANTS** are well and truly wedged on. Love ya! #sorrynotsorry

To my Female Success Network sisters, Moments friends and clients that have been part of this journey with me, I am humbled when I think of the privilege it has been to learn from you and that our lives connected when they did. Thank you for putting your faith and trust in me, I salute you.

To my gorgeous friends and family, I love you.

To Mum, your favourite quote will always be within everything I do, I promise to always; 'live well, laugh often, love much...'

And finally, to my husband, Andy. My soulmate, best friend, my everything. Thank you for your unwavering support in everything I do, even when I drive you insane with a new idea most days. Without you and the love we have created, all my wildest dreams wouldn't be possible. Thank you for always allowing me to pursue what makes my heart sing and believing in our dreams for the future. I love you to the moon and back, always and forever.

REFERENCES & RESOURCES

SHOP

Throughout the book I refer to using candles and scent to stimulate your senses, evoke feelings, emotions and to enhance your home with items which set the right mood to create the ambience you desire. To help you achieve this, I have created a bespoke range of luxury fragrances, candles and diffusers in collaboration with Moments Candles Co which you can find at: www.chooseyourmoments.com or simply scan the quick response code on the top of next page:

LEARN MORE

To learn more about your personal energy number, access all of the additional tools, tutorials and resources which will enhance your experience of Creative Feng Shui, visit: www.sarahstone.com/book-resources or simply scan the quick response code below:

BOOKS, RESEARCH & INSPIRING PEOPLE MENTIONED

The One Thing, Book by Gary Keller & Jay Papasan,
www.The1Thing.com

Marie Diamond, Feng Shui Master,
www.MarieDiamond.com

Nichola Sproson, Founder, Intuitive Alignment Method,
www.NicholaSproson.com

Kezia Luckett, Creator of Mind Conditioning Therapy,
www.KeziaLuckett.com

Tony Robbins, International Motivational Speaker,
www.TonyRobbins.com

The Spruce, Inspirational Blog & Articles,
www.TheSpruce.com

DISCLAIMER

Anything suggested to try in this book is merely suggested for educational and inspirational purposes. If you choose to undertake a project, home alteration or any other suggestion found in these pages, you will be doing so at your own risk and your own responsibility.

Sarah Stone and Creative Feng Shui by Sarah Stone cannot and will not be responsible for errors, misplacements or omissions. Although this data is thoroughly researched, well vetted for its accuracy, and given every effort to provide the most factual information possible has been applied.

In addition, Sarah is not a magician and cannot and does not promise you money, fame, power, marriage, good health or anything else; she can only guarantee to provide you with ancient Feng Shui principles as well as empowerment tools and other exercises, ideas and inspiration to enhance spaces and help them to feel and look better.

In addition, because Sarah's approach to Creative Feng Shui is unique in many senses, if you are inspired to write on a topic, please credit the ideas appropriately.

Sarah Stone is the voice and founder of Creative Feng Shui. She helps her clients around the world create powerful activations for success, wealth, health and happiness in their home, life and business.

A successful entrepreneur and multiple business owner who has been featured in Forbes for her contributions to other female entrepreneurs, Sarah has always been guided to help others find their version of success.

Creative Feng Shui is now her gift to help others more intentionally create goals that will enable them to live a life they love, activate success and become a magnet in attracting their wildest desires.

Sarah has been referred to, many times, as 'the best kept secret in town' and she is also well known for being the secret weapon in highly acclaimed business owners, high achievers and celebrity's success.

She is on a mission to help more people master this essential element of intentional living and wants to share her unique formula in transforming the energy flow of your living and working spaces to shape your life in incredible ways.

Sarah is based between New York and the United Kingdom with an international portfolio of clientele.

www.sarahstone.com

facebook.com/sarahstoneonline

twitter.com/sarahstonecom

instagram.com/sarahstoneonline

pinterest.com/sarahstoneonline

linkedin.com/in/sarah-stone

AFTERWORD

Hey you did it! Congratulations! You made it to the end of the book and have now received everything you need to start living with more intention. It feels like we've explored such a wide landscape of intrigue, inspiration and insight into Creative Feng Shui.

It's been such a privilege to share my perspective on how you can truly start to 'Live What You Love'. I hope this marks the start of positive change and influence in your life, home, business and relationships so that you can welcome everything you desire and more.

I hope this marks the start of new beginnings, limitless success and a wonderful journey for you. I am so grateful that you have taken the time to read this book, from the bottom of my heart, THANK YOU.

If you feel empowered to take even more inspired action, there is more to come. If you would like to explore some of the topics on a deeper level, you can join me over on my website (www.sarahstone.com) where I will continually be creating articles, tools and resources for you to enhance your Creative Feng Shui skills and know-how. I hope you'll join me and together we can see what unfolds.

Until then, I wish you limitless fortune, joy, success and prosperity; whatever that looks like for you!

Remember, everything you could ever possibly need is within you, I believe in you.

With love and light,

Sarah xx

Printed in Great Britain
by Amazon